DATE DUE

JAN 4 '79 DEC 8 73			

JOSTEN'S 30 508

Meetings

Meetings
Martin Buber

Edited with an introduction and
bibliography by Maurice Friedman

1973
Open Court Publishing Company
La Salle, Illinois

Contents

Introduction

Meetings—no autobiography but, as Martin Buber himself insisted, only autobiographical fragments—is one of Buber's little classics. It is different in kind but equal in quality to his famous poetic-philosophic work *I and Thou* and to *The Way of Man*—his quintessential distillation of the wisdom contained in the tales of the Hasidim. In contrast to these two books, *Meetings* was produced as a collection of small pieces written in very different periods of Buber's life. It came into being as part of *The Philosophy of Martin Buber*, edited by Paul Arthur Schilpp and Maurice Friedman, published by Open Court in 1967, a prodigious volume that was ten years in the making. It was the twelfth volume in the distinguished *Library of Living*

Philosophers series and the only volume in the entire series in which Professor Schilpp worked with a coeditor. The unique pattern of these volumes is to begin each one with an intellectual autobiography written by a world-famous philosopher, which is then followed by twenty or thirty essays on this philosopher written by his best-known critics, and then followed by a section written by the philosopher himself in which he replies to each critic. In the most recent volume on philosopher Karl Popper, the autobiography ran to some two hundred fifty pages of closely knit personal intellectual history. Though one of the great philosophers and universal geniuses of his time and certainly one of the best-read men of the century, Martin Buber, in contrast, confined himself to fragments that can best be described by the title of his 1917 book *Events and Meetings*.

Some of these fragments were already written and in a number of cases published here and there in Buber's writings. Others he wrote especially for this occasion. In 1958 while Buber was studying and teaching at Princeton University and again in 1960, during the four months that I spent in Jerusalem doing research for my book *Problematic Rebel*, Martin Buber and I together selected the personal anecdotes for the *"Autobiographical Fragments"* and ordered them according to chronology, significance, and their place in the body of the text or the appendix. Often I suggested the fragment in the first place, then Buber responded, deciding whether he was willing to include it and if so in what fullness or with what omissions. In other cases he selected the fragment or wrote it for the first time.

These "events and meetings" are in the fullest sense of the term "teaching" and perhaps, in the end, the most real teaching that Martin Buber has left us. "I am no philosopher, prophet, or theologian," Buber said at a celebration of his eightieth birthday, "but a man who has seen something and who goes to a window and points to what he has seen." In the highly significant Foreword to his Hasidic chronicle-novel *For the Sake of Heaven*, Buber wrote: "He who hopes for a teaching from me that is anything other than a pointing of this sort will always be disappointed." If we take this statement seriously, and I think we must, then even Buber's formal philosophical anthropology, such as *Between Man and Man* and *The Knowledge of Man,* must be understood not as the comprehensive *Weltanschauung,* or worldview, of the monological philosopher but as response and address in the dialogue that took place between Buber and the situations and thinkers that he encountered and that takes place between Buber and his reader. This is still more the case in Buber's works of poetical philosophy, such as *Daniel: Dialogues of Realization* and *I and Thou,* in his works of literature, such as *The Tales of Rabbi Nachman, The Legend of the Baal-Shem, For the Sake of Heaven,* and his "mystery play" *Elijah,** in his translation and interpretations of the Hebrew Bible, and in his interpretations of the teachings and retelling of the legends of Hasidism—the popular communal Jewish mysticism of eighteenth- and nineteenth-century Eastern Europe. Of these last *The Way of Man according to the Teaching of the Hasidim,*** each section of which takes off from the interpretation of a Hasidic tale, and Buber's two volumes of *The Tales of the Hasidim* are especially illuminating in this respect. They point and teach through the recounting of concrete stories to which we can return again and again to test the insights and feelings that have arisen in response to them. These stories have often served my wife and myself as the basis for "basic encounter-discussion" workshops and classes. Not only can one discover which tales "speak to his condition," but also the hidden teaching contained in the restraint with which Buber retells these "legendary anecdotes" and in the order in which he has arranged them.

This same teaching as pointing awaits those who bring themselves into genuine dialogue with the *"Autobiographical Fragments."* I have myself often used them—in everything from graduate seminars and undergraduate classes to Esalen encounter groups and Pendle Hill courses—as the basis for highly meaningful group discussion and interaction. When people discuss abstractions, they regularly pass one another by without even knowing it. With these "events and meetings," in contrast, there is a check on "mismeeting"—the concrete facts of each story itself plus the checks the group places upon that reading in, or projecting of, our own feelings and assumptions that most of us do even without being aware of it. At the same time, the light plays freely upon one aspect after another of each anecdote, like the sparkle of many-faceted diamonds, and each person finds his or her unique relationship to the story. The sharing of this relationship enriches the happening in the group and turns even the simplest event into one pregnant with meaning.

We may ask, for example, what is the connection between the poignant story of Buber's mother, who leaves him at the age of four, the word "mismeeting" that recurs throughout this story, and the strange conclusion that it was through this experience that Buber first began to understand genuine meeting. I have never discussed this question with a group without something new being revealed to me that I should never have thought of by myself. Again in the anecdote of "The School" a fruitful discussion may center around the question of the connection between the experience of participating "eight long years" as a "thing in a sacral event in which no dram of my person could or would take part" and the opposition to all missionary efforts that Buber claims arose—not from any attempt at conversion or any intolerance or persecution—but from just this experience. In the sequel on "The Two Boys" the thoughtful reader must ask him or herself what the master meant when he said to the young Buber, "You are a good boy, you will help us," what Buber meant when he wanted to scream, "Help? Help whom?" and why and how this convulsion of Buber's childhood served as the beginning of the long series of lessons that taught Buber that true moral command is wed not to maxim but to situation, not to obedience, which splits the obeying self in half, but to the response of the whole person. Few readers will fail to be astonished by the fact that at the age of fourteen the question about the infinity of space and time nearly drove young Martin to suicide and still more by the fact that it was Kant's "Prologemana to Any Future Metaphysics" that saved him. Nor to be intrigued by the "seduction" of the seventeen-year old by Nietzsche's Zarathustra and his overcoming of that seduction in favor of an altogether different understanding of time and eternity. Nor can one read unmoved the account of Buber's "hero worship" of the German socialist Ferdinand Lassalle or fail to be struck by the mystery of the way in which Bach—sung and played as Bach would have wished to have been sung and played—modified the "ground tone" of Buber's life and helped him in his Lassalle crisis that engendered his "insight into the problematic reality of human existence and into the fragile possibility of doing justice to it."

How could I forget the excitement of discovery in my own writings on Buber*** as one field after another opened before me—from education and social philosophy to psychotherapy and religious symbolism—as I attempted to systematize Buber's thought and seek out its implications and significance? Or my coming to the conviction that the real heart of Buber's philosophy—and of the "lived concrete" about which he was so concerned—is found not in conceptual or systematic thought but in the four-dimensional reality of events and meetings? This conviction I owe in large part to these "Autobiographical Fragments."

By the same token, the full significance of many of these "Meetings" can only be grasped in the context in which I shall present them in *Martin Buber: A Critical Biography*. "The Cause and the Person," for example, belongs to Buber's early Zionist activity and to the relationship between Buber and his Nietzschean hero Theodor Herzl—a tension of loyalty and independence that illuminates the central tragic relationship between the Yehudi and the Seer in *For the Sake of Heaven*. Again "The Zaddik" belongs to Buber's lifelong task of interpreting and retelling the teachings and tales of the Hasidim as well as to the period of his "Talks on Judaism" and the Prague Bar Kochba Circle. "Question and Answer" and "A Conversion" belong to the fateful period of the First World War—the twelve years the impact of which Buber himself described as one great experience of faith in which all the doors and windows of his being sprang open and the storm blew through every nook and cranny. To this period, too, belongs the one "Autobiographical Fragment" that I tried in vain to persuade Buber to write—the story of his profound response to the news that his friend Gustav Landauer had been kicked to death on the way from one prison to another after he was arrested on false charges following the fall of the socialist *Raterepublik* in Munich in whose government he had taken part. After more than forty years Buber still found himself "too close" to this all-important event to be able to write about it, and I have had to piece it together in the chapter of my biography devoted to Landauer. "Report on Two Talks" belongs to the period directly after the First World War when Buber and his friends turned to adult education as the one hope for reclaiming Germany and reaching the people. "Samuel and Agag" is illuminated by the deeply moving story of Buber's friendship and coworking with Franz Rosenzweig in the unique translation of the Hebrew Bible that preserves its elemental oral quality.

None of this implies, however, that these fragments do not stand by themselves. On the contrary, some of the most profound of Buber's hard-won insights are contained within them like a vein of gold in marble. They await extraction by those who wrestle and contend with them until they are compelled to divulge their secret. The thought concerning "dark charisma" at the end of "The Cause and the Person" touches on Buber's deepest trust—that in the "God of the sufferers" who dwells with the *zaddik,* the justified man, in his suffering and who places himself in the hands of that secret history that, in contrast to every political success, transmutes the world anonymously and silently from the depths.

That a similar thought is expressed in Buber's essay on "China and Us" (*A Believing Humanism*) in terms of the Taoist teaching of *wu-wei*—the action of the whole being that appears to be inaction—in no way diffuses the concentrated force of this mystery, any more than the fusion of biblical, Hasidic, and Taoist teaching in Buber's classic *I and Thou*. Nor is it surprising that in "The Zaddik" Buber shows a very different sort of leader from Herzl—one responsible for each individual person who comes before him, one who measures the sounding lead of responsibility each hour anew with his words and his person. Although this kind of leader is more and more the person Buber himself became, we cannot doubt the anguished authenticity of Buber's disclaiming cry, "I who am truly no *zaddik,* no one assured in God, rather a man endangered before God, a man wrestling ever anew for God's light, ever anew engulfed in God's abysses."

"The Walking Stick and the Tree" is astonishing because, in this preface to Buber's beautiful but still not fully mature mystical-existential work *Daniel,* there already appears in unmistakable form that knowledge about "inclusion," or "experiencing the other side of the relationship," that has made Buber's philosophy of dialogue so much more concrete and fruitful than any of the other formulations of the "I-Thou" philosophy in our age. And the inability to believe in a God about whom one can speak in the third person which dawns on Buber in "Question and Answer" brings to light that witness for speaking *to* the "eternal Thou" and not *about* it to which Buber remained true in every line that he wrote in the forty years of life left to him. It was this unwavering life-stance that compelled the great Protestant theologian Paul Tillich to testify a month after Buber's death that one could not speak of God as an object in Buber's presence.

The story "A Conversion," already famous from the essay "Dialogue" in *Between Man and Man,* belongs together with "Question and Answer" as the twin testimony to the illegitimacy of the separation of the relation between man and God and that between man and man. Martin Buber himself considered his main contribution to human thought to lie in the fact that he had thus united Kierkegaard's "I-Thou" relationship between the "Single One" and the Transcendent with Ludwig Feuerbach's "I-Thou" relationship within the interhuman. The full significance of the setting of these two tales within the period of the First World War only comes through when both tales are taken together. This becomes especially clear if the reader refrains from following Meyer Levin, Aubrey Hodas, and other "Buber experts" in jumping to the conclusion that the young man in "The Conversion" committed suicide. How much more meaningful it is in our age of world wars, extermination camps, and atomic explosions that, as Buber himself wrote me, "He died at the front out of a despair that did not oppose his own death"! Having understood that, we can tackle the difficult question of in what lay the existential guilt that Buber experienced in "The Conversion." Certainly it was not his failure to remove the young man's despair. Buber wrote me that the great Czech novelist Franz Kafka came to see him several times in 1911 and that he was really an unhappy man. Yet Buber in no way implied any sense of guilt over being unable to relieve Kafka's unhappiness. Nor was it simply his failure to guess the question the young man did not ask that constituted Buber's guilt. Two months before Buber's own death another young man came to see him with an important life-question. But he left it to Buber to carry on both sides of the dialogue, assuming that he would understand his question without having to ask it. The young man in "The Conversion," in contrast, did not look to Buber as the magic helper who would reach into his soul and extract his question. He did not simply *have* a question: he concentrated his whole being into *becoming* a question. It was the address of this unspeakable question that Buber might have heard behind every question that Herr Méhé *did* ask if Martin Buber had been "present in spirit"—if he had brought himself into the dialogue with the whole of his being, rather than with the intellectual and social fragments left over from his preoccupation with his morning of mystic ecstasy.

The first of Buber's "Report on Two Talks," that with the worker, raises one of the most important questions possible concerning a philosophy such as Buber's which reports what was experienced as "Thou" in the language of "It." If Buber could not go with this worker to his factory and "win his trust in real life-relationship," neither could he, even while living, go with the countless readers throughout the world who also encountered his pointing to the Thou through the philosophical language of It. Was the failure of dialogue, then, chiefly the fault of the worker who accepted Buber's pointing to the Thou as just another *Weltanschauung,* or world-view? Or was it Buber's attempt to shatter the security of the worker's naturalistic world-view, hoping thus to force him to move into the openness of dual-voiced *dialogue* in response to Buber's own use of single-voiced *dialectic?* Or was it both? And what, on the other hand, made the dialogue real in the second of the two talks, that with the noble old philosopher Paul Natorp, when no agreement was reached even about the use of terms? The Christian reader will also ask himself the significance of Buber's inversion of Jesus' saying, "When two or three are together in my name, I shall be present," into "When two or three are truly together, they are together in the name of God." "Let us be friends" in this second talk is really "Let us say thou to each other" in the original German. The latter expression seemed to me so lacking in meaning to the English-speaking reader that I sought a cultural equivalent when I translated this anecdote for *Eclipse of God.*

If "Samuel and Agag" throws light on Buber's lifelong relationship to the Hebrew Bible, it also shows the way in which he walked the "narrow ridge" between the universalism of orthodoxy, on the one hand, and that of liberalism, on the other, preserving the tension of the unique and of the "lived concrete." It also illustrates the other central *Leitmotiv* of Buber's thought—"holy insecurity." That Buber walked this "narrow ridge" of "holy insecurity" in his life and not just in his philosophy these "Autobiographical Fragments" show with a power that none of his other writings can equal. It is no accident that he concludes them with the beautiful little statement of "Books and Men" in which he rejects the soft white bread of the spirit for the hard crust of human relationship on which he bites his teeth out. If Buber was occupied with a fourth revision of his translation of the Bible until the coma which led to his death, it was nonetheless true that he died without books, "with another human hand in my own." Surely this concern for human contact was the main reason why he insisted on leaving the hospital in order that he might die at home.

Meetings: Fragments of An Autobiography has already been published for some years as a separate book in Germany, Holland, Israel, and Japan. It is to be hoped that with these Open Court editions this unique classic will find the widespread distribution and response that it deserves in the English-speaking world.

Chapter 7, "The Horse," and Chapter 15, "A Conversion" are reprinted from the essay "Dialogue" and Appendix I, "Beginnings," is reprinted from "The History of the Dialogical Principle" both in Martin Buber, *Between Man and Man,* all three selections with the permission of The Macmillan Company. Chapter 12, "The Zaddik," is reprinted from Buber's *Hasidism and Modern Man* with the permission of The Horizon Press. Chapter 13, "The Walking Stick and the Tree," is reprinted from Buber's *Daniel: Dialogues of Realization* with the permission of Holt, Rinehart, Winston, & Co. Chapter 16, "Report on Two Talks," is reprinted from Buber's *Eclipse of God* and Appendix III, "Books and Men," is reprinted from Buber's *Pointing the Way,* both with the permission of Harper & Row. Chapter 11, "The Cause and the Person," and Appendix II, "A Tentative Answer," were both published previously in book form in the

German original. The rest of the chapters were written specifically for *The Philosophy of Martin Buber* volume of *The Library of Living Philosophers,* the English edition of which was published in 1963 by the Open Court Publishing Company in America and Cambridge University Press in England. (There have also been German and Japanese editions of this volume.) "The Horse" and "A Conversion" were translated by Ronald Gregor Smith. All other sections of *Meetings,* both those written especially for *The Philosophy of Martin Buber* and those reprinted from previously published books, including "The History of the Dialogical Principle" in *Between Man and Man,* were translated from the German by me.

Dr. Maurice Friedman,
Swarthmore, Pennsylvania, July, 1973

* *Elijah* can be found in English only as part of Maurice Friedman, *Martin Buber and the Theater* (New York: Funk & Wagnalls, 1969).

** *The Way of Man* can be obtained as a separate paperback or as Book Four of Martin Buber, *Hasidism and Modern Man,* ed. & trans. with An Introduction by Maurice Friedman (New York: Harper Torchbooks, 1966).

*** Maurice Friedman, *Martin Buber: The Life of Dialogue* (Chicago: The University of Chicago Press, London: Routledge & Kegan Paul, 1955; rev. paperback ed. New York: Harper Torchbooks, 1960), and Maurice Friedman, *Martin Buber: A Critical Biography* (New York: E. P. Dutton, London: Collins Ltd., 1974).

Meetings

1. *My Mother*

It cannot be a question here of recounting my personal life (I do not possess the kind of memory necessary for grasping great temporal continuities as such), but solely of rendering an account of some moments that my backward glance lets rise to the surface, moments that have exercised a decisive influence on the nature and direction of my thinking.

The earliest memory which has this character for me stems out of my fourth year of life. About a year before that the separation of my parents broke up the home of my childhood in Vienna (still today I see with closed eyes the Danube canal under the house, the sight of which I used to enjoy with a feeling of certainty that nothing could happen to me). At that time I had been brought to my grandparents on my father's side near Lvov (Lemberg), then the capital city of the Austrian "crownland" Galicia. They were both people of high rank, noble persons in the exact sense of the term and, in a special manner, suited to and supplementing each other. They were both disinclined to talk over the affairs of their own existence. Of what had taken place between my parents, nothing, of course, was spoken in my presence; but I suspect that it was also hardly ever a subject of discussion between them, except in practical and unavoidable connection. The child itself expected to see its mother again soon; but no question passed its lips. Then there took place at one time what I have to tell here.

The house in which my grandparents lived had a great rectangular inner courtyard surrounded by a wooden balcony extending to the roof on which one could walk around the building at each floor. Here I stood once in my fourth year with a girl several years older, the daughter of a neighbor, to whose care my grandmother had entrusted me. We both leaned on the railing. I cannot remember that I spoke of my mother to my older comrade. But I hear still how the big girl said to me: "No, she will never come back." I know that I remained silent, but also that I cherished no doubt of the truth of the spoken words. It remained fixed in me; from year to year it cleaved ever more to my heart, but after more than ten years I had begun to perceive it as something that concerned not only me, but all men. Later I once made up the word "*Vergegnung*"—"mismeeting," or "miscounter"—to designate the failure of a real meeting between men. When after another twenty years I again saw my mother, who had come from a distance to visit me, my wife, and my children, I could not gaze into her still astonishingly beautiful eyes without hearing from somewhere the word "*Vergegnung*" as a word spoken to me. I suspect that all that I have learned about the genuine meeting in the course of my life had its first origin in that hour on the balcony.

2. *My Grandmother*

My grandmother Adele was one of those Jewesses of a certain period who, in order to create freedom and leisure for their husbands to study the Torah, managed the business with circumspect zeal. For my grandfather "study of the teaching" had a special significance. Although an autodidact, he was a genuine philologist who is to be thanked for the first, and today still the authoritative, critical edition of a special class of Hebrew literature: the Midrashim—a unique mixture of interpretation of the Bible, wise sayings, and rich saga. In his civil occupation he was a great landowner, in addition a corn-merchant and the owner of phosphorite mines on the Austrian-Russian border. Beyond this he belonged to the number of the leading men of the Jewish community and to those of the town's chamber of commerce, experienced men with a judgment of their own. He never neglected these honorary offices; his own business, however, he left in general to his wife who conducted it all in a splendid and circumspect manner, but made no decision without consulting her spouse.

Among the Jews in the small Galician town where my grandmother grew up the reading of "alien" literature was proscribed, but for the girls all readings, with the exception of edifying popular books, were held unseemly. As a fifteen-year-old she had set up for herself in the storehouse a hiding place in which stood volumes of Schiller's periodical "*Die Horen*," Jean Paul's book on education, *Levana*, and many other German books which had been secretly and thoroughly read by her. When she was seventeen years old, she took them and the custom of concentrated reading with her into her marriage, and she reared her two sons in the respect for the authentic word that cannot be paraphrased. The same influence she later exercised on me. I learned even before I was fourteen (at that time I moved into the house of my father and my stepmother) what it means really to express something. I was affected in a special manner by the way that this woman handled the large-size, similarly bound copy books in which she recorded everyday income and expenditures: in between these entries she registered, after she had spoken them half aloud to herself, the passages which had become important to her out of her readings. Now and then she set down her own comments as well, which in no way imitated the style of the classic but from time to time stated something that she had to reply in intercourse with the great spirits. The same was true of her oral utterances: even when she obviously communicated the conclusion of a reflection, it had the appearance of something perceived. That undoubtedly came from the fact that with her, experiencing and reflecting on experience were not two stages but, as it were, two sides of the same process: when she looked at the street, she had at times the profile of someone meditating on a problem, and when I found her all alone in meditation, it seemed to me at times as if she listened. To the glance of the child, however, it was already unmistakable that when she at times addressed someone, she really addressed him.

My grandfather was a true philologist, a "lover of the word," but my grandmother's love for the genuine word affected me even more strongly than his: because this love was so direct and so devoted.

3. *Languages*

I went to school for the first time when I was ten years old. Up till then I received private tutoring, chiefly in languages, both because of my own inclination and talents and because for my grandmother a language-centered humanism was the royal road to education.

The multiplicity of human languages, their wonderful variety in which the white light of human speech at once fragmented and preserved itself, was already at the time of my boyhood a problem that instructed me ever anew. In instructing me it also again and again disquieted me. I followed time after time an individual word or even structure of words from one language to another, found it there again and yet had time after time to give up something there as lost that apparently only existed in a single one of all the languages. That was not merely "nuances of meaning": I devised for myself two-language conversations between a German and a Frenchman, later between a Hebrew and an ancient Roman and came ever again, half in play and yet at times with beating heart, to feel the tension between what was heard by the one and what was heard by the other, from his thinking in another language. That had a deep influence on me and has issued in a long life into ever clearer insight.

My knowledge of languages as a boy also made it possible for me at times to provide my grandfather, whom I went to visit daily from my father's house, with a little help at his work. Thus it happened, for instance, that in reading "Rashi" (Rabbi Shlomo Yizhaki), the great Bible and Talmud exegete of the eleventh century, my grandfather found a text explained through a reference to a French turn of speech and asked me how this was to be understood. I had at times to deduce from the Hebrew transcription the old French wording and now to make this understandable first to myself, then to my grandfather. Later, however, when I sat alone in my room in my father's house, I was oppressed by the question: What does it mean and how does it come about that one "explains" something that was written in one language? The world of the Logos and of the Logoi opened itself to me, darkened, brightened, darkened again.

4. *My Father*

From about the ninth year on I spent each summer on the estate of my father, and at fourteen I moved from my grandfather's house to my father's townhouse.

The influence of my father on my intellectual development was of a different kind from that of my grandparents. It did not derive at all from the mind.

In his youth my father had had strong intellectual interests; he had occupied himself seriously with the questions that had been raised in such books as Darwin's *Origin of the Species* and Renan's *Life of Jesus*. But already early he dedicated himself to agriculture and devoted ever more of himself to it. Soon he was an exemplary phenomenon in the East Galician landed property.

When I was still a child, he brought with him from the Paris International Exhibition a great packing of breeding eggs of a type of hen still unknown in the east; he held it on his knees the whole long journey in order that no harm might come to it. Thirty-six years he worked with all kinds of implements whose specific effects he carefully tested in order to heighten the productivity of his soils.

He had mastered the technique of his age in his domain. But I noticed what really concerned him when I stood with him in the midst of the splendid herd of horses and observed him as he greeted one animal after the other, not merely in a friendly fashion but positively individually, or when I drove with him through the ripening fields and looked at them as he had the wagon halt, descended and bent over the ears again and again, in order finally to break one and carefully taste the kernels. This wholly unsentimental and wholly unromantic man was concerned about genuine human contact with nature, an active and responsible contact. Accompanying him thus on his way at times, the growing boy learned something that he had not learned from any of the many authors that he read.

In a special way the relationship of my father to nature was connected with his relationship to the realm that one customarily designates as the social. How he took part in the life of all the people who in one or another manner were dependent on him: the laborers attached to the estate, in their little houses that surrounded the estate buildings, houses built according to his design, the little peasants who performed service for him under conditions worked out with exact justice, the tenants; how he troubled about the family relationships, about the upbringing of children and schooling, about the sickness and aging of all the people—all that was not derived from any principles. It was solicitude not in the ordinary, but in the personal sense, in the sense of active responsible contact that could rise here to full reciprocity. In the town too my father did not act otherwise. To sightless charity he was fiercely averse; he understood no other help than that from person to persons, and he practiced it. Even in his old age he let himself be elected to the "bread commission" of the Jewish community of Lemberg and wandered tirelessly around the houses in order to discover the people's real wants and necessities; how else could that take place except through true contact!

One thing I must still mention. My father was an elemental story-teller. At times in conversation, just as its way led him, he told of people whom he had known. What he reported of them there was always the simple occurrence without any embroidery, nothing further than the existence of human creatures and what took place between them.

5. *The School*

My school was called "Franz Josef's Gymnasium." The language of instruction and of social intercourse was Polish, but the atmosphere was that, now appearing almost unhistorical to us, which prevailed or seemed to prevail among the peoples of the Austro-Hungarian empire: mutual tolerance without mutual understanding. The pupils were for the largest part Poles, in addition to which there was a small Jewish minority (the Ruthenians had their own schools). Personally the pupils got on well with one another, but the two groups as such knew almost nothing about each other.

Before 8 o'clock in the morning all the pupils had to be assembled. At 8 o'clock the signal bell sounded. One of the teachers entered and mounted the professor's lecturing desk, above which on the wall rose a large crucifix. At the same moment all the pupils stood up in their benches. The teacher and the Polish students crossed themselves; he spoke the Trinity formula, and they prayed aloud together. Until one might sit down again, we Jews stood silent and unmoving, our eyes glued to the floor.

I have already indicated that in our school there was no perceptible hatred of the Jews; I can hardly remember a teacher who was not tolerant or did not wish to pass as tolerant. But the obligatory daily standing in the room resounding with the strange service affected me worse than an act of intolerance could have affected me. Compulsory guests, having to participate as a thing in a sacral event in which no dram of my person could or would take part, and this for eight long years morning after morning: that stamped itself upon the life-substance of the boy.

No attempt was ever made to convert any of us Jewish pupils; yet my antipathy to all missionary activity is rooted in that time. Not merely against the Christian mission to the Jews, but against all missionarizing among men who have a faith with roots of its own. In vain did Franz Rosenzweig try to win me for the idea of a Jewish mission among the non-Jews.

6. *The Two Boys*

The classroom included five rows with six benches apiece. At each bench two pupils sat.

The Two Boys

The furthest bench to the left, at the window, through which one saw nothing else but the almost empty square for play and sports, belonged to me and my best friend. For eight years we sat at this same bench, he to the left, I to the right.

The recesses in the teaching lasted a full quarter of an hour as a rule. When the weather was in some measure favorable, the whole school band used to storm out to the square and stay there in zealous activity until the signal bell. When the weather was all too adverse, we remained together in the classroom, but only on special occasions did a larger group form. Ordinarily the structure was only loose; a few youths stood telling things or discussing together, and the composition of these small groups changed according to the different themes that emerged from one time to the next.

Once, however, in a fall utterly spoiled by rain (in the winter before I had become twelve) a special change took place that continued for some weeks.

In the third bench of the middle row sat two boys who until then had in no wise struck me and probably also had not struck most of the others as unusual. Now, however, they drew all glances to themselves. Day after day they conducted for us, without leaving the bench, mimic games with clownlike agility. They made no sound, and their faces remained unalterably severe. After some time the game took on an ever more penetratingly sexual character. Now the faces of the two looked, I imagined, as souls in the pains of hell, about which some of my fellow pupils knew enough to report to me in the tone of experts. All movements were cruelly forced. We stared at the two as long as the spectacle lasted. Shortly before the end of the recess they broke off. In our conversations the occurrence was never mentioned.

A few weeks after the spectacles had taken on this character, I was called to the school director. He received me with the gentle friendliness that we knew in him as something unalterable and asked me at once what I knew of the activities of the two. "I know nothing!" I screamed. He spoke again, just as gently as before. "We know you well," he said to me; "you are a good child, you will help us." "Help? Help whom?" I wanted—so it seems to me—to reply; but I remained silent, I stared silently at the director. Of what else happened almost nothing has penetrated into my memory, only that a great weeping as never before overcame me, and I was led away almost unconscious. A few hours later, however, when I tried at home to remember the last look of the director, it was not a gentle, but a frightened look that met me.

I was kept home for a few days, then I returned to school. The third bench of the middle row was empty and remained so until the end of the school year.

The long series of experiences that taught me to understand the problematic relationship between maxim and situation, and thereby disclosed to me the nature of the true norm that commands not our obedience but ourselves, had begun with this convulsion of my childhood.

7. *The Horse*

When I was eleven years of age, spending the summer on my grandparents' estate, I used, as often as I could do it unobserved, to steal into the stable and gently stroke the neck of my darling, a broad dapple-gray horse. It was not a casual delight but a great, certainly friendly, but also deeply stirring happening. If I am to explain it now, beginning from the still very fresh memory of my hand, I must say that what I experienced in touch with the animal was the Other, the immense otherness of the Other, which, however, did not remain strange like the otherness of the ox and the ram, but rather let me draw near and touch it. When I stroked the mighty mane, sometimes marvellously smooth-combed, at other times just as astonishingly wild, and felt the life beneath my hand, it was as though the element of vitality itself bordered on my skin, something that was not I, was certainly not akin to me, palpably the other, not just another, really the Other itself; and yet it let me approach, confided itself to me, placed itself elementally in the relation of *Thou* and *Thou* with me. The horse, even when I had not begun by pouring oats for him into the manger, very gently raised his massive head, ears flicking, then snorted quietly, as a conspirator gives a signal meant to be recognizable only by his fellow-conspirator; and I was approved. But once—I do not know what came over the child, at any rate it was childlike enough—it struck me about the stroking, what fun it gave me, and suddenly I became conscious of my hand. The game went on as before, but something had changed, it was no longer the same thing. And the next day, after giving him a rich feed, when I stroked my friend's head he did not raise his head. A few years later, when I thought back to the incident, I no longer supposed that the animal had noticed my defection. But at the time I considered myself judged.

8. *Philosophers*

In that early period of my life, philosophy twice, in the form of two books, entrenched directly upon my existence—in my fifteenth and in my seventeenth year.

The two events do not allow themselves to be inserted into the process of appropriating a philosophical education, which was established in particular on a thorough reading of Plato (Greek was my favorite language). They were events which broke through the continuity—the presupposition of all genuine educational work—catastrophic events. In the first of them the philosophy confronted the catastrophic situation, delivering and helping. In the second the philosopher not only stirred me up but transported me into a sublime intoxication. Only after a long time was I able to escape this intoxication completely and attain to a certainty of the real.

Of the first of these two events I have told elsewhere, but it is of importance to me to interpret still more clearly something of what was reported there.

It says in that passage:

A necessity I could not understand swept over me: I had to try again and again to imagine the edge of space, or its edgelessness, time with a begin-ning and an end or a time without beginning or end, and both were equal-ly impossible, equally hopeless—yet there seemed to be only the choice between the one or the other absurdity.

Here it must be added above all that at that time the question about time had oppressed me in a far more tormenting fashion than that about space. I was irresistibly driven to want to grasp the total world process as actual, and that meant to understand it, "time," either as beginning and ending or as without beginning and end. At each attempt to accept them as reality, both proved equally absurd. If I wanted to take the matter seriously (and I was ever again compelled to want just this), I had to transpose myself either to the beginning of time or to the end of time. Thus I came to feel the former like a blow in the neck or the latter like a rap against the forehead—no, there is no beginning and no end! Or I had to let myself be thrown into this or that bottomless abyss, into infinity, and now everything whirled. It happened thus time after time. Mathematical or physical formulae could not help me; what was at stake was the reality of the world in which one had to live and which had taken on the face of the absurd and the uncanny.

Then a book came into my hand, Kant's *Prolegomena*. In it was taught that space and time are "nothing more than formal conditions of our sensory faculty," are "not real properties that adhere to the things in themselves" but "mere forms of our sensory perception."

This philosophy exercised a great quieting effect on me. Now I needed no longer, tormented, to inquire of time a final time. Time was not a sentence hanging over me; it was mine, for it was "ours." The question was explained as unanswerable by its nature, but at the same time I was liberated from it, from having to ask it. Kant's present to me at that time was philosophical freedom.

About two years after that the other book took possession of me, a book that was, to be sure, the work of a philosopher but was not a philosophical book: Nietzsche's *Thus Spake Zarathustra*. I say "took possession of me," for here a teaching did not simply and calmly confront me, but a willed and able—splendidly willed and splendidly able—utterance stormed up to and over me. This book, characterized by its author as the greatest present that had ever been made to mankind up till then, worked on me not in the manner of a gift but in the manner of an invasion which deprived me of my freedom, and it was a long time until I could liberate myself from it.

Nietzsche himself wished "the basic conception" of his book to be understood as an interpretation of *time*: its interpretation as "eternal return of the same," that is, as an infinite sequence of finite periods of time, which are like one another in all things so that the end phase of the period goes over into its own beginning. This conception, evaluated by its proclaimer as the most abysmal teaching, is no teaching at all but the utterance of an ecstatically lived-through possibility of thought played over with ever new variations. The "Dionysian" pathos has by no means been transformed here into a philosophical one, as Nietzsche already early had in mind. It has remained Dionysian, as its modern variant, produced by the enthusiasm of the Dionysian man over his own heights and depths.

Kant had not undertaken to solve the sense-confusing riddle that is set us by the being of time; he completed the philosophical limitation of it in that he made it into a problem of we ourselves being referred to the form of time. Nietzsche, who wanted to have nothing to do with philosophical self-moderations, set in the place of one of the primal mysteries of time—the manifest mystery of the uniqueness of all happening—the pseudo-mystery of the "eternal return of the same." Although the boy of seventeen did not and could not accept this conception, there still took place in his spirit a, so to speak, negative seduction. As he appears to me in my memory, after so many years—through Kant, who understood time as the form of "our" perception, the way could open to him to ask the question: "But if time is only a form in which we perceive, where *are* 'we'? Are we not in the timeless? Are we not in eternity?" By that, of course, a wholly other eternity is meant than the circular one which Zarathustra loves as "fatum." What is meant is what is incomprehensible in itself, that which sends forth time out of itself and sets us in that relationship to it that we call existence. To him who recognizes this, the reality of the world no longer shows an absurd and uncanny face: because eternity is. That the entrance to this way long remained closed to me is to be traced to a certain, not insignificant, extent to that fascination by "Zarathustra."

9. *Vienna*

I spent my first year of university studies in Vienna, the city of my birth and my earliest childhood. The detached, flat memory images appear out of the great corporal context like slides of a magic lantern, but also many districts that I could not have seen address me as acquaintances. This original home of mine, now foreign, taught me daily, although still in unclear language, that I had to accept the world and let myself be accepted by it; it was indeed ready to be accepted. Something was established at that time that in later years could not become recast through any of the problematics of the age.

The lectures of those two semesters, even the significant scholarly ones, did not have a decisive effect on me. Only some seminars into which I had prematurely flung myself, rather the seminary as such, immediately exerted a strong influence: the regulated and yet free intercourse between teacher and students, the common interpretations of texts, in which the master at times took part with a rare humility, as if he too were learning something new, and the liberated exchange of question and answer in the midst of all scholastic fluency—all this disclosed to me, more intimately than anything that I read in a book, the true actuality of the spirit, as a "between."

What affected me most strongly, however, was the Burgtheater into which at times, day after day, I rushed up three flights after several hours of "posting myself " in order to capture a place in the highest gallery. When far below in front of me the curtain went up and I might then look at the events of the dramatic agon as, even if in play, taking here and now, it was the word, the "rightly" spoken human word that I received into myself, in the most real sense. Speech here first, in this world of fiction as fiction, won its adequacy; certainly it appeared heightened, but heightened to itself. It was only a matter of time, however, until—as always happened—someone fell for a while into recitation, a "noble" recitation. Then, along with the genuine spokenness of speech, dialogical speech or even monological (in so far as the monologue was just an addressing of one's own person as a fellow man and no recitation), this whole world, mysteriously built out of surprise and law, was shattered for me—until after some moments it arose anew with the return of the over-against.

Since then it has sometimes come to pass, in the midst of the casualness of the everyday, that, while I was sitting in the garden of an inn in the countryside of Vienna, a conversation penetrated to me from a neighboring table (perhaps an argument over falling prices by two market wives taking a rest), in which I perceived the spokeness of speech, sound becoming "Each-Other."

10. *A Lecture*

My third semester, during which I completed my twentieth year, I spent in Leipzig.

What had the strongest effect on me there was undoubtedly hearing Bach's music, and in truth Bach's music so sung and played—of that I was certain at that time and have remained certain—as Bach himself wished that it be sung and played. But it would be fruitless for me to undertake to say, indeed, I cannot even make clear to myself—in what way Bach has influenced my thinking. The ground-tone of my life was obviously modified in some manner and through that my thinking as well. In general I am not at all in the position, in these autobiographical fragments, to report on such great and mysterious things. In its stead I shall tell here of a small incident that took place then and, as it later proved, was not unimportant.

I had for some time occupied myself with the talks and writings of Ferdinand Lassalle and with his biography too. I admired his spiritual passion and his readiness, in personal as in public life, to stake his existence. What was manifestly problematic in his nature went unnoticed; it did not even concern me. When a Socialist club whose meetings I had attended a few times invited me to deliver a lecture, I decided to speak about Lassalle and did so. The lecture that I delivered was the image of a hero after the model of Carlyle. I pointed to a destiny that was intended for tragedy from the beginning. This tragedy was manifested in the path of his work—the failure of his undertaking to lay the foundation of a new society—but also in that of his life up till his absurd and yet symbolically significant death.

When I had finished, the applause was great. Then an old man came up to me. He was, as he at once communicated to me, a tailor by trade and had in his youth belonged to Lassalle's most intimate circle. He seized my hand and held it fast for a long time. Then he looked at me enthusiastically and said: "Yes! Thus, thus he was!"

An almost tender feeling came over me: "How good it is to be confirmed thus!" But even at that moment a fright suddenly fell upon me and pierced through my thoughtless joy: "No, it is I who have been the confirmer, the lying confirmer of an idol!"

The true, hidden, cast aside, issue of my Lassalle studies revealed itself in a flash: the knowledge of the unmanageable contradiction that had burned in a bold and vain heart and out of it had been hurled into the human world. I stammered a salutation to the friendly tailor and fled.

In the following weeks I sought, with the most inadequate means and with the lack of success that was its due, to substitute for the smashed hero's bust a kind of analytical representation: this proved to be an only seemingly legitimate simplification. Slowly, waveringly, grew the insight into the problematic reality of human existence and into the fragile possibility of doing justice to it. Bach helped me.

11. *The Cause and the Person*

It was at the Sixth Zionist Congress, 1902, Herzl had just launched the thunder of his denunciation against the opposition; he had answered the criticism of Davis Trietsch, less with factual arguments than with personal counter-criticism in which he dealt with Trietsch's own colonizing activities. The chief thrust was a record that had been taken down from a "victim" of this activity.

(It must be mentioned here that in the days after this incident I was a member of what was virtually a board of arbitration appointed by the Congress. That board decided, by a vote of three to two—I was one of the minority—to issue no detailed statement on the result of its investigations, but some details may be made public today.)

Apart from the fact that this thrust was directed against the person rather than against his cause, it was not executed with a correct sword; the "victim" was no victim, and the record—well, it was a record. . . . Herzl swung his weapon in good faith; no doubt existed about that. But he had not examined it closely enough beforehand.

After his speech Herzl retired into his conference room. Berthold Feiwel and I soon followed him there to point out, as friends of Trietsch, the untenable nature of his accusations, and to demand the appointment of a committee to make an inquiry into them. As we walked the short distance to the conference room, I was profoundly perturbed. I had already, indeed, since the previous Congress, stood in decisive opposition to Herzl, but this opposition had been wholly objective, and I had not ceased for a moment to have faith in the man. Now, for the first time, my soul revolted—so violently that I still have a physical recollection of it. When I entered the room, however, my agitation was in an instant transformed by the sight that met me, and the heart that had just been pounding grew numb.

Only Herzl and his mother were in the room. Frau Jeannette sat in an armchair, silent and unmoving, but her face and eyes shining with the most lively sympathetic participation—splendid in sympathy as I had known once in my grandmother. Herzl was pacing up and down the room with long strides, exactly like a caged lion. His vest was unbuttoned, his breast rose and fell; I had never dreamed that he, whose gestures were always mastered and masterly, could breathe so wildly. It was only later that I noticed his pallor, so strongly did his eyes flash and burn.

It became at once compellingly clear to me that here it was impossible to remain inwardly the representative of one side. Outside, in the hall, was a man, my friend and ally, who had been hurt, who had suffered a public injustice. But here was the author of the injustice, whose blow had dealt the wound—a man who, though misled, was still my leader, sick with zeal; a man consumed with zeal for his faith: his faith in his cause and in himself, the two inextricably bound together.

I was twenty-four years of age and this was perhaps the first time that I set foot on the soil of tragedy where there is no longer such a thing as being in the right. There was only one thing to learn that was greater still: how out of the grave of being in the right the right is resurrected. But this is something I only learned many years later.

Our task had become inwardly impracticable: for speaking to this man opposite, one could only essentially appeal from "his cause," which he so lived, to the—truth of his cause, and who could do that? But, of course, we carried out our task: we pointed out, demanded what we were authorized and obliged to point out and demand.

Herzl continued to pace up and down the room, giving no sign that he was listening. Occasionally I glanced at his mother—her face had darkened; there was something there that terrified me, I did not know what it was, but it was there.

Suddenly, however, Herzl stopped before us, and spoke to us. His tone was by no means what we might have expected—it was a passionate but smiling tone, although there was no smile on his lips. "I would have taken him to task in a wholly different way!" he exclaimed. "Wholly differently! But there before the platform, directly opposite me, a girl—his fiancée, I have heard—placed herself; there she stood, her eyes flashing at me. A wonderful person, I tell you! I could not do it!"

And now his mouth, too, smiled, as though liberated. And who could have refrained from smiling with him? The charmer "Told" smiled in his romantic way; I, undoubtedly, smiled too, like a schoolboy who has discovered that Horace meant real

friends and real sweethearts, and even on the once more brightened face of the old—no, not old at all—gentlewoman in the
armchair there was a smile, such as I have only observed in the
Jewish women of that generation. The secret of that smile has
been lost.

It was no longer possible to reply. In the light of the non-
objectivity of his confession concerning the reason for his
forbearance, the non-objectivity of his attack naturally seemed
even more grave. And yet...! We discharged our task,
everything now going off smoothly, impersonally, without dif-
ficulties of any sort and we took our leave. This was the last time
that I saw Herzl at such close quarters.

Then I did not want to recollect that image, but since
then—after the angel had done his work, the angel whose
nameless presence had at that time frightened Herzl's mother and
me—I have often thought over that occasion.

What, indeed, was Theodor Herzl's attitude toward the cause
and the person? And how is it in general with these two, "cause"
and "person"?

That to Herzl his cause was indissolubly bound up with his
person—this fact manifested itself clearly enough in his fight
against Ahad Ha-am when he summoned us young men, who in
that situation stood on the side of his opponent, to "find our way
back to *the movement*." Probably this is the case with most of the
men who act in history. His fundamental view was certainly that
there was little sense in discussing principles and methods, since,
in the final analysis, everything depends not upon them, but upon
the person to whom their realization and application is entrusted,
in other words: upon the individual who uses them, and by means
of them serves. Serves whom? Just the cause that is indissolubly
bound up with the person? We appear to be reasoning in a circle.

But let us regard the problem from the other side, from the
side of the people. Let us consider, for example, the concept of
Max Weber, according to whom genuine democracy means to ap-

point a leader whom one trusts and to follow him as long as he accomplishes his task, but if he fails, to call him to account, to judge him, to depose him, even "To the gallows with him!" The cause, therefore, is bound up with the person as long as his *charisma*, i.e., his power of leadership, to use Weber's term, proves effective. From this point of view we can understand Herzl's attitude toward his critics; it is charismatic. This is why he does not say: "You are wrong, for matters stand thus and so," but rather: "You are wrong, for you are not the man to do this properly—you lack the *charisma*."

But is this concept right or wrong? It cannot be set aside by a cheap ideology composed of a mediocre policy and a mediocre morality. The "history of the world" so far attests to it. Only our hope for a different leadership and a different following, for a truly dialogical relationship between the two, contests it. In any case, the categories of the objective and the subjective, with which we are so familiar, do not in truth hold for the problem that has opened up to us.

But the fiancée with the flashing eyes! Is this not certainly a dreadful lack of objectivity? I do not know. Perhaps through the impression that his opponent had one, even if only one human being who would take his part *thus*, Herzl had been gripped by the question whether there might not be yet another reality, different from that of obvious world history—a reality hidden and powerless because it has not come into power; whether there might not be, therefore, men with a mission who have not been called to power and yet are, in essence, men who have been summoned; whether excessive significance has not perhaps been ascribed to the circumstances that separate the one class of men from the other; whether success is the only criterion; whether the unsuccessful man is not destined at times to gain a belated, perhaps posthumous, perhaps even anonymous victory which even history refuses to record: whether, indeed, when even this does not happen, a blessing is not spoken, nonetheless, to these abandoned ones, a word that confirms them; whether there does not exist a "dark" charisma. The man who acts in history does not allow himself to be overwhelmed by such questions, for if he did so, he would have to despair, and to withdraw. But the moments in which they touch him are the truly religious moments of his life.

12. *The Zaddik*

In my childhood I spent every summer on an estate in Bukovina. There my father took me with him at times to a nearby village of Sadagora. Sadagora is the seat of a dynasty of "*zaddikim*" (*zaddik* means righteous, proven), that is, of Hasidic rabbis. There no longer lives in the present-day community that high faith of the first Hasidim, that fervent devotion which honored in the *zaddik* the perfected man in whom the immortal finds its mortal fulfillment. Rather the present-day Hasidim turn to the *zaddik* above all as the mediator through whose intercession they hope to attain the satisfaction of their needs. Even in these degenerate Hasidim there still continues to glow, in the unknown ground of their souls, the word of Rabbi Eliezar that the world was created for the sake of the perfected man (the *zaddik*), even though there should be only one.

This I realized at that time, as a child, in the dirty village of Sadagora from the "dark" Hasidic crowd that I watched—as a child realizes such things, not as thought, but as image and feeling—that the world needs the perfected man and that the perfected man is none other than the true helper. Certainly, the power entrusted to him has been misinterpreted by the faithful, had been misused by himself. But is it not at base a legitimate, the legitimate power, this power of the helping soul over the needy? Does there not lie in it the seed of future social orders?

At any rate, in a childish fashion, these questions already dawned on me at that time. And I could compare on the one side with the head man of the province whose power rested on nothing but habitual compulsion; on the other with the rabbi, who was an honest and God-fearing man, but an employee of the "directorship of the cult." Here, however, was another, an incomparable; here was, debased yet uninjured, the living double kernel of humanity: genuine *community* and genuine *leadership*.

The palace of the *rebbe*, in its showy splendor, repelled me. The prayer house of the Hasidim with its enraptured worshipers seemed strange to me. But when I saw the *rebbe* striding through the rows of the waiting, I felt, "leader," and when I saw the Hasidim dance with the Torah, I felt "community." At that time there rose in me a presentiment of the fact that common reverence and common joy of soul are the foundations of genuine human community.

In 1910 or 1911, in Bukovina, not far from Sadagora, after a lecture that I had delivered, I went, with some members of the association that had arranged the evening, into a coffee house. I like to follow the speech before many, whose form allows no reply, with a conversation with a few in which person acts on person and my view is set forth directly through going into objection and question.

We were just discussing a theme of moral philosophy when a well-built middle-aged Jew of simple appearance came up to the table and greeted me. To my no doubt somewhat distant return greeting, he replied with words not lacking a slight reproof: "Doctor! Do you not recognize me?" When I had to answer in the negative, he introduced himself as M., the brother of a former steward of my father's. I invited him to sit with us, inquired about his circumstances of life and then took up again the conversation with the young people. M. listened to the discussion, which had just taken a turn toward somewhat abstract formulations, with eager attentiveness. It was obvious that he did not understand a single word; the devotion with which he received every word resembled that of the believers who do not need to know the content of a litany since the arrangement of sounds alone gives them all that they need, and more than any content could.

After a while, nonetheless, I asked him whether he had perhaps something to say to me; I should gladly go to one side with him and talk over his concern. He vigorously declined. The conversation began again and with it M.'s listening. When another half hour had passed, I asked him again whether he did not perhaps have a wish that I might fulfill for him; he could count on me. No, no, he had no wish, he assured me. It had grown late; but, as happens to one in such hours of lively interchange, I did not feel weary; I felt fresher, in fact, than before, and decided to go for a walk with the young people. At this moment M. approached me with an unspeakably timid air. "Doctor," he said, "I should like to ask you a question." I bid the students wait and sat down with him at a table. He was silent. "Just ask, Mr. M.," I encouraged him; "I shall gladly give you information as best I can." "Doctor," he said, "I have a daughter." He paused; then he continued, "And I also have a young man for my daughter." Again a pause. "He is a student of law. He passed the examinations with distinction." He paused again, this time somewhat longer. I looked at him encouragingly; I supposed that he would entreat me to use my influence in some way on behalf of the presumptive son-in-law. "Doctor," he asked, "is he a steady man?" I was surprised, but felt that I might not refuse him an answer. "Now, Mr. M.," I explained, "after what you have said, it can certainly be taken for granted that he is industrious and able." Still he questioned further. "But Doctor," he said, "does he also have a good head?"—"That is even more difficult to answer," I replied; "but at any rate he has not succeeded with industry alone, he must also have something in his head." Once again M. paused; then he asked, clearly as a final question, "Doctor, should he now become a judge or a lawyer?"—"About that I can give you no information," I answered. "I do not know the young man, indeed, and even if I did know him, I should hardly to able to advise in this matter." But then M. regarded me with a glance of almost melancholy renunciation, half-complaining, half-understanding, and spoke in an indescribable tone, composed in equal part of sorrow and humility: "Doctor, you do not *want* to say—now, I thank you for what you have said to me."

As a child, I had received an image of the *zaddik* and through the sullied reality had glimpsed the pure idea, the idea of the genuine leader of a genuine community. Between youth and manhood this idea had arisen in me through knowledge of Hasidic teaching as that of the perfected man who realizes God in the world. But now in the light of this droll event, I caught sight in my inner experience of the *zaddik's* function as a leader. I who am truly no *zaddik*, no one assured in God, rather a man endangered before God, a man wrestling ever anew for God's light, ever anew engulfed in God's abysses, nonetheless, when asked a trivial question and replying with a trivial answer, then experienced from within for the first time the true *zaddik*, questioned about revelations and replying in revelations. I experienced him in the fundamental relation of his soul to the world: in his responsibility.

13. *The Walking Stick and the Tree*

After a descent during which I had to utilize without a halt the late light of a dying day, I stood on the edge of a meadow, now sure of the safe way, and let the twilight come down upon me. Not needing a support and yet willing to afford my lingering a fixed point, I pressed my walking stick against a trunk of an oak tree. Then I felt in twofold fashion my contact with being: here, where I held the stick, and there, where it touched the bark. Apparently only where I was, I nonetheless found myself there too where I found the tree.

At that time dialogue appeared to me. For the speech of man is like that stick wherever it is genuine speech, and that means: truly directed address. Here, where I am, where ganglia and organs of speech help me to form and to send forth the word, here I "mean" him to whom I send it, I intend him, this one unexchangeable man. But also there, where he is, something of me is delegated, something that is not at all substantial in nature like that being here, rather pure vibration and incomprehensible; that remains there, with him, the man meant by me, and takes part in the receiving of my word. I encompass him to whom I turn.

14. *Question and Answer*

It was in May of the year 1914 (my wife and I and our two children, now had already lived some eight years in a suburb of Berlin) when Reverend Hechler, whom I had not seen for a long time, called me. He was just in Berlin and would like to visit me. Soon afterward he came.

I had become acquainted with Hechler in the autumn of 1899 in a railroad carriage. The much older man began a conversation with me in which we soon learned that we shared the same views. Through a real eschatological belief in the living Christ, he stood close to the Zionist movement to which I then had belonged for a short time. The return of the Jewish people to their homeland was to him the promised presupposition of the return of Christ. He journeyed just then to the Grand Duke of Baden to whom he had a short time before introduced Herzl. He had been an educator of princes and was highly esteemed in many European courts.

Question and Answer

In the course of the conversation I handed to Hechler the manuscript of a "hymn" to the awakening Jewish people which I had written shortly before. This hymn filled him with such enthusiasm (entirely without basis) that he declared that he must read it to the Grand Duke. Soon afterward he had not merely done this but had published the questionable little opus without my knowledge. When I opened the door of my Berlin dwelling to Hechler, I was struck by how aged, but also by how upright he was. After the warm mutual greeting, he drew forth from one of the gigantic pockets of his havelock a bundle of papers wrapped in a blue-white cloth. Out of it, first of all, he pulled forth the manuscript together with the proofs of that poem of 1899, but then a large sheet that he slowly unfolded. It was a graphic representation of the prophecy of Daniel on which he indicated to me, as if on a map of a historical period, the exact point in which we just now found ourselves. Then he spoke somewhat as follows: "Dear friend! I come from Athens (he had earlier been the teacher of the Greek princes, among others). I have stood on the spot where Paul spoke to the Athenians of the unknown God. And now I come to you to say to you that in this year the world war will break out."

The certainty which was expressed in this sentence stemmed, as I have only later understood, out of a peculiar fusion of spheres: the believing interpretation of Daniel had been mixed and concretized with material flowing to it from the courts of Europe, without an awareness of what took place thus in the depths of the soul having penetrated into that consciousness. But what struck me most forcibly in the sentence that he spoke was the word "world war" which I heard then for the first time. What kind of a "war" was that—so I asked myself although still by no means clearly enough—which embraced the "world"? Clearly something essentially different at any rate from what one had formerly called "war"! From that hour dates the presentiment that has from then

43

on grown in me, that the historical time of "wars" was over and something different, only seemingly of that same nature, but becoming ever more different and ever more monstrous, was getting ready to swallow history and with it men.

Hechler stayed a few hours with us. Then I accompanied him to the railway station. In order to get there, one first had to go to the end of the small street of the "colony," in which we lived and then on a narrow path covered with coal-dust, the so-called "black path" along the railroad tracks. When we had reached the corner where the colony street met this path, Hechler stood still, placed his hand on my shoulder and said: "Dear friend! We live in a great time. Tell me: Do you believe in God?" It was a while before I answered, then I reassured the old man as best I could: He need have no concern about me in this matter. Upon this I brought him to the railway station and installed him in his train.

When I now returned home, however, and again came to that corner where the black path issued into our street, I stood still. I had to ponder to the depths of the matter. Had I said the truth? Did I "believe" in the God whom Hechler meant? What was the case with me? I stood a long time on the corner determined not to go further before I had found the right answer.

Suddenly in my spirit, there where speech again and again forms itself, there arose without having been formulated by me, word for word distinct:

"If to believe in God means to be able to talk about him in the third person, then I do not believe in God. If to believe in him means to be able to talk to him, then I believe in God." And after a while, further: "The God who gives Daniel such foreknowledge of this hour of human history, this hour before the 'world war,' that its fixed place in the march of the ages can be foredetermined, is not my God and not God. The God to whom Daniel prays in his suffering is my God and the God of all."

I remained standing for a long while on the corner of the black path and gave myself up to the clarity, now beyond speech, that had begun.

15. *A Conversion*

In my earlier years the "religious" was for me the exception. There were hours that were taken out of the course of things. From somewhere or other the firm crust of everyday was pierced. Then the reliable permanence of appearances broke down; the attack which took place burst its law asunder. "Religious experience" was the experience of an otherness that did not fit into the context of life. It could begin with something customary, with consideration of some familiar object, but which then became unexpectedly mysterious and uncanny, finally lighting a way into the lightning-pierced darkness of the mystery itself. But also, without any intermediate stage, time could be torn apart—first the firm world's structure, then the still firmer self-assurance flew apart and you were delivered to fullness. The "religious" lifted you out. Over there now lay the accustomed existence with its affairs, but here illumination and ecstasy and rapture held without time or sequence. Thus your own being encompassed a life here and a life beyond, and there was no bond but the actual moment of the transition.

The illegitimacy of such a division of the temporal life, which is streaming to death and eternity and which only in fulfilling its temporality can be fulfilled in face of these, was brought home to me by an everyday event, an event of judgment, judging with that sentence from closed lips and an unmoved glance such as the ongoing course of things loves to pronounce.

What happened was no more than that one forenoon, after a morning of "religious" enthusiasm, I had a visit from an unknown young man, without being there in spirit. I certainly did not fail to let the meeting be friendly, I did not treat him any more remissly than all his contemporaries who were in the habit of seeking me out about this time of day as an oracle that is ready to listen to reason. I conversed attentively and openly with him—only I omitted to guess the questions which he did not put. Later, not long after, I learned from one of his friends—he himself was no longer alive—the essential content of these questions; I learned that he had come to me not casually, but borne by destiny, not for a chat but for a decision. He had come to me; he had come in this hour. What do we expect when we are in despair and yet go to a man? Surely a presence by means of which we are told that nevertheless there is meaning.

Since then I have given up the "religious" which is nothing but the exception, extraction, exaltation, ecstasy; or it has given me up. I possess nothing but the everyday out of which I am never taken. The mystery is no longer disclosed, it has escaped or it has made its dwelling here where everything happens as it happens. I know no fullness but each mortal hour's fullness of claim and responsibility. Though far from being equal to it, yet I know that in the claim I am claimed and may respond in responsibility, and know who speaks and demand a response.

I do not know much more. If that is religion then it is just *everything,* simply all that is lived in its possibility of dialogue. Here is space also for religion's highest forms. As when you pray you do not thereby remove yourself from this life of yours but in your praying refer your thought to it, even though it may be in order to yield it; so too in the unprecedented and surprising, when you are called upon from above, required, chosen, empowered, sent, you with this your mortal bit of life are meant. This moment is not extracted from it, it rests on what has been and beckons to the remainder that has still to be lived. You are not swallowed up in a fullness without obligation, you are willed for the life of communion.

16. *Report on Two Talks*

I shall tell about two talks. One apparently came to a conclusion, as only occasionally a talk can come, and yet in reality remained unconcluded; the other was apparently broken off and yet found a completion such as rarely falls to the lot of discussions.

Both times it was a dispute about God, about the concept and the name of God, but each time of a very different nature.

On three successive evenings I spoke at the adult folk-school of a German industrial city on the subject "Religion as Reality." What I meant by that was the simple thesis that "faith" is not a feeling in the soul of man but an entrance into reality, an entrance into the *whole* reality without reduction and curtailment. This thesis is simple but it contradicts the usual way of thinking. And so three evenings were necessary to make it clear, and not merely three lectures but also three discussions which followed the lectures. At these discussions I was struck by something that bothered me. A large part of the audience was evidently made up of workers but none of them spoke up. Those who spoke and raised questions, doubts, and reflections were for the most part students (for the city had a famous old university). But all kinds of other circles were also represented; the workers alone remained silent. Only at the conclusion of the third evening was this silence, which had by now become painful for me, explained. A young worker, came up to me and said: "Do you know, we can't speak in there, but if you would meet with us tomorrow, we could talk together the whole time." Of course I agreed.

The next day was a Sunday. After dinner I went to the agreed place and now we talked together well into the evening. Among the workers was one, a man no longer young, whom I was drawn to look at again and again because he listened as one who really wished to hear. Real listening has become rare in our time. It is found most often among workers who are not indeed concerned about the person speaking, as is so often the case with the bourgeois public, but about what he has to say. This man had a curious face. In an old Flemish altar picture representing the adoration of the shepherds, one of them, who stretches out his arms toward the manger, has such a face. The man in front of me did not look as if he might have any desire to do the same;

47

moreover, his face was not open like that in the picture. What was notable about him was that he heard and pondered, in a manner as slow as it was impressive. Finally, he opened his lips as well. "I have had the experience," he explained slowly and impressively, repeating a saying which the astronomer Laplace is supposed to have used in conversation with Napoleon, "that I do not need this hypothesis 'God' in order to be quite at home in the world." He pronounced the word "hypothesis" as if he attended the lectures of the distinguished natural scientist who had taught in that industrial and university city and had died shortly before. Although he did not reject the designation "God" for his idea of nature, that naturalist spoke in a similar manner whether he pursued zoology or *Weltanschauung*.

The brief speech of the man struck me; I felt myself more deeply challenged by him than the others. Up till then we had certainly debated very seriously, but in a somewhat relaxed way; now everything had suddenly become severe and hard. How should I reply to the man? I pondered awhile in the now severe atmosphere. It came to me that I must shatter the security of his *Weltanschauung*, through which he thought of a "world" in which one "felt at home." What sort of a world was it: What we were accustomed to call world was the "world of the senses," the world in which there exists vermilion and grass-green, C major and B minor, the taste of apple and of wormwood. Was this world anything other than the meeting of our own senses with those unapproachable events about whose essential definition physics always troubles itself in vain? The red that we saw was neither there in the "things," nor here in the "soul." It at times flamed up and glowed just so long as a red-perceiving eye and a red-engendering "oscillation" found themselves over against each other. Where then was the world and its security? The unknown "objects" there, the apparently so well known and yet not graspable "subjects" here, and the actual and still so evanescent meeting of both, the "phenomena"—was that not already three worlds which could no longer be comprehended from one alone?

How could we in our thinking place together these worlds so divorced from one another? What was the being that gave this "world," which had become so questionable, its foundation?

When I was through a stern silence ruled in the now twilit room. Then the man with the shepherd's face raised his heavy lids, which had been lowered the whole time, and said slowly and impressively, "You are right."

I sat in front of him dismayed. What had I done? I had led the man to the threshold beyond which there sat enthroned the majestic image which the great physicist, the great man of faith, Pascal, called the God of the Philosophers. Had I wished for that? Had I not rather wished to lead him to the other, Him whom Pascal called the God of Abraham, Isaac, and Jacob, Him to whom one can say Thou?

It grew dusk, it was late. On the next day I had to depart. I could not remain, as I now ought to do; I could not enter into the factory where the man worked, become his comrade, live with him, win his trust through real-life relationship, help him to walk with me the way of the creature who *accepts* the creation. I could only return his gaze.

Some time later I was the guest of a noble old thinker. I had once made his acquaintance at a conference where he gave a lecture on elementary folk-schools and I gave one an adult folk-schools. That brought us together, for we were united by the fact that the work "folk" has to be understood in both cases in the same all-embracing sense. At that time I was happily surprised at how the man with the steel-gray locks asked us at the beginning of his talk to forget all that we believed we knew about his philosophy from his books. In the last years, which had been war years, reality had been brought so close to him that he saw everything with new eyes and had to think in a new way. To be old is a glorious thing when one has not unlearned what it means to *begin;* this old man had even perhaps first learned it thoroughly in old age. He was not at all young, but he was old in a young way, knowing how to begin.

He lived in another university city situated in the west. When the theology students of that university invited me to speak about prophecy, I stayed with the old man. There was a good spirit in his house, the spirit that wills to enter life and does not prescribe to life where it shall let it in.

One morning I got up in order to read proofs. The evening before I had received galley proofs of the preface of a book of mine, and since this preface was a statement of faith, I wished to read it once again quite carefully before it was printed. Now I took it into the study below that had been offered to me in case I should need it. But here the old man already sat at his writing-desk. Directly after greeting me he asked me what I had in my hand, and when I told him, he asked whether I would not read it aloud to him. I did so gladly. He listened in a friendly manner but clearly astonished, indeed with growing amazement. When I was through, he spoke hesitatingly, then, carried away by the importance of his subject, ever more passionately. "How can you bring yourself to say 'God' time after time? How can you expect that your readers will take the word in the sense in which you wish it to be taken? What you mean by the name of God is something above all human grasp and comprehension, but in speaking about it you have lowered it to human conceptualization. What word of human speech is so misused, so defiled, so desecrated as this! All the innocent blood that has been shed for it has robbed it of its radiance. All the injustice that it has been used to cover has effaced its features. When I hear the Highest called 'God,' it sometimes seems almost blasphemous."

The kindly eyes flamed. The voice itself flared. Then we sat silent for awhile facing each other. The room lay in the flowing brightness of early morning. It seemed to me as if a power from the light entered into me. What I now answered, I cannot today reproduce but only indicate.

"Yes," I said, "it is the most heavy-laden of all human words. None has become so soiled, so mutilated. Just for this reason I may not abandon it. Generations of men have laid the burden of their anxious lives upon this word and weighed it to the ground; it lies in the dust and bears their whole burden. The races of man with their religious factions have torn the word to pieces; they have killed for it and died for it, and it bears their finger-marks and their blood. Where might I find a word like it to describe the Highest! If I took the purest, most sparkling concept from the inner treasure-chamber of the philosophers, I could only capture thereby an unbinding product of thought. I could not capture the presence of Him whom the generations of men have honored and degraded with their awesome living and dying. I do indeed mean Him whom the hell-tormented and heaven-storming generations of men mean. Certainly, they draw caricatures and write 'God' underneath; they murder one another and say 'in God's name.' But when all madness and delusion fall to dust, when they stand over against Him in the loneliest darkness and no longer say 'He, He' but rather sigh 'Thou,' shout 'Thou,' all of them the one word, and when they then add 'God,' is it not the real God whom they all implore, the One Living God, the God of the children of man? Is it not He who *hears* them? And just for this reason is not the word 'God' the word of appeal, the word which has become a *name*, consecrated in all human tongues for all times? We must esteem those who interdict it because they rebel against the injustice and wrong which are so readily referred to 'God' for authorization. But we may not give it up. How understandable it is that some suggest we should remain silent about the 'last things' for a time in order that the misused words may be redeemed! But they are not to be redeemed *thus*. We cannot cleanse the word 'God' and we cannot make it whole; but, defiled and mutilated as it is, we can raise it from the ground and set it over an hour of great care."

It had become very light in the room. It was no longer dawning, it was light. The old man stood up, came over to me, laid his hand on my shoulder and spoke: "Let us be friends." The conversation was completed. For where two or three are truly together, they are together in the name of God.

17. *Samuel and Agag*

I once met on a journey a man whom I already knew through an earlier meeting. He was an observant Jew who followed the religious tradition in all the details of his life-pattern. But what was for me essential (as had already become unmistakably clear to me at that first meeting) was that this relationship to tradition had its origin and its constantly renewed confirmation in the relationship of the man to God.

When I now saw him again, it turned out that we fell into a discussion of biblical questions, and indeed not of peripheral questions but central ones, central questions of faith. I do not know exactly any longer in what connection we came to speak of that section of the Book of Samuel in which it is told how Samuel delivered to King Saul the message that his dynastic rule would be taken from him because he had spared the life of the conquered prince of the Amalekites. I reported to my partner in dialogue how dreadful it had already been to me when I was a boy to read this as the message of God (and my heart compelled me to read it over again or at least to think about the fact that this stood written in the Bible). I told him how already at that time it horrified me to read or to remember how the heathen king went up to the prophet with the words on his lips, "Surely the bitterness of death is past," and was hewn to pieces by him. I said to my partner: "I have never been able to believe that this is a message of God. I do not believe it."

With wrinkled forehead and contracted brows, the man sat opposite me and his glance flamed into my eyes. He remained silent, began to speak, became silent again. "So?" he broke forth at last, "so? You do not believe it?" "No," I answered, "I do not believe it." "So? so?" he repeated almost threateningly. "You do not believe it?" And I once again: "No." "What . . . what . . . ,"—he thrust the words before him one after the other—"what do you believe then?" "I believe," I replied without reflecting, "that Samuel has misunderstood God." And he, again slowly, but more softly than before: "So? You believe that?" And I: "Yes." Then we were both silent. But now something happened the like of which I have rarely seen before or since in this my long life. The angry countenance opposite me became transformed, as if a hand had passed over it soothing it. It lightened, cleared, was now turned toward me bright and clear. "Well," said the man with a positively gentle tender clarity, "I think so too." And again we became silent, for a good while.

There is in the end nothing astonishing in the fact that an observant Jew of this nature, when he has to choose between God and the Bible, chooses God: the God in whom he believes, Him in whom he can believe. And yet, it seemed to me at that time significant and still seems so to me today. The man later came to the land of Israel and here I met him once again, some time before his death. Naturally I regarded him then as the speaker of that word of one time; but in our talk the problem of biblical belief was not touched on. It was, indeed, no longer necessary.

For me, however, in all the time since that early conversation the question has again and again arisen whether at that time I expressed in the right manner what I meant. And again and again I answered the question in the same way: Yes and No. Yes in so far as it concerns what had been spoken of in that conversation; for there it was right to answer my partner in his language and within the limits of his language in order that the dialogue might not come to naught and that the common insight into one truth at times afforded to two men might fulfill itself, in no matter how limited a way. In so far as it concerns that, Yes. But No when it concerns both recognizing oneself and making known that man and the human race are inclined to misunderstand God. Man is so created that he can understand, but does not have to understand, what God says to him. God does not abandon the created man to his needs and anxieties; He provides him with the assistance of His word; He speaks to him, He comforts him with His word. But man does not listen with faithful ears to what is spoken to him. Already in hearing he blends together command of heaven and statute of earth, revelation to the existing being and the orientations that he arranges himself. Even the holy scriptures of man are not excluded, not even the Bible. What is involved here is not ultimately the fact that this or that form of biblical historical narrative has misunderstood God; what is involved is the fact that in the work of throats and pens out of which the text of the Old Testament has arisen, misunderstanding has again and again attached itself to understanding, the manufactured has been mixed with the received. We have no objective criterion for the distinction; we have only faith—when we have it. Nothing can make me believe in a God who punishes Saul because he has not murdered his enemy. And yet even today I still cannot read the passage that tells this otherwise than with fear and trembling. But not it alone. Always when I have to translate or to interpret a biblical text, I do so with fear and trembling, in an inescapable tension between the word of God and the words of man.

18. *Beginnings*

The question of the possibility and reality of a dialogical relationship between man and God, thus of a free partnership of man in a conversation between heaven and earth whose speech in address and answer is the happening itself, the happening from above and the happening from below, had already accosted me in my youth. In particular since the Hasidic tradition had grown for me into the supporting ground of my own thinking, hence, since about 1905, that had become an innermost question for me. In the language of the writings on the dialogical principle that arose many years later, it appears emphatically for the first time in the autumn of 1907 in the introduction to my book, *The Legend of the Baal-Shem*. This introduction was concerned with the radical distinction between myth in the narrower sense (the myth of the mythologists) and legend. It said:

The legend is the myth of the calling. In pure myth there is no difference of being. . . . Even the hero only stands on another rung than the god, not over against him; they are not the I and the Thou. . . . The god of pure myth does not call, he begets; he sends forth the begotten, the hero. The god of the legend calls, he calls the son of man: the prophets, the saints. . . . The legend is the myth of I and Thou, of caller and called, of the finite that enters into the infinite and of the infinite that needs the finite.

Here the dialogical relationship is thus exemplified in its highest peak: because even on this height the essential difference between the partners persists unweakened, while even in such nearness the independence of man continues to be preserved.

From this event of the exception, of the extraction, however, my thought now led me, ever more earnestly, to the common that can be experienced by all. The clarification took place first of all here too in connection with my interpretation of Hasidism: in the "Preface" written in September 1919 to my book, *Der Grosse Maggid und seine Nachfolge* (1922), the Jewish teaching was described as "wholly based on the two-directional relation of human I and divine Thou, on reciprocity, on the *meeting*." Soon after, in the autumn of 1919, followed the first, still unwieldy draft of *I and Thou*.

There now followed two years in which I could do almost no work except on Hasidic material, but also—with the exception of Descartes' *Discours de la methode* which I again took up—read no *philosophica* (therefore the works connected with the subject of dialogue by Cohen, Rosenzweig, and Ebner I read only later, too late to affect my own thought). This was part of a procedure that I understood at that time as a spiritual askesis. Then I was able to begin the final writing of *I and Thou,* which was completed in the spring of 1922. As I wrote the third and last part, I broke the reading-askesis and began with Ebner's fragments. His book showed me, as no other since then, here and there in an almost uncanny nearness, that in this our time men of different kinds and traditions had devoted themselves to the search for the buried treasure. Soon I also had similar experiences from other directions.

Of the initiators I had already as a student known Feuerbach and Kierkegaard; Yes and No to them had become a part of my existence. Now there surrounded me in spirit a growing circle of men of the present generation who were concerned, even if in unequal measure, about the one thing that had become for me an ever more vital matter. The basic view of the twofold nature of the human attitude is expressed in the beginning of *I and Thou.* But I had already prepared the way for this view in the distinction presented in my book *Daniel* (1913) between an "orienting," objectifying basic attitude and a "realizing," making present one. This is a distinction that coincides in its core with that carried through in *I and Thou* between the I-It relation and the I-Thou relation, only the latter is no longer grounded in the sphere of subjectivity but in the sphere between the beings. But this is the decisive transformation that took place in a series of spirits in the time of the First World War. It announced itself in very manifold meanings and spheres, but the fundamental connection between them, stemming out of the disclosed transformation of the human situation, is unmistakable.

19. *A Tentative Answer*
(Jerusalem, May 1955)

Asked about a tentative answer that might then be the chief
conclusion expressible in conceptual language of my experiences
and observations, I can give no other reply than confess to the
knowledge comprehending the questioner and myself: to be man
means to be *the* being that is over-against. The insight into this
simple fact has grown in the course of my life. It has been expressed in diverse other theses of like subject and similar construction,
and I certainly hold many of them to be not incorrect; my knowing leads to just this, however, that it is this over-againstness
that matters.

In this thesis the definite article is fully accentuated. All
beings in nature are indeed placed in a being-with-others, and in
each living being this enters as perception of others and action
toward others in work. But what is peculiar to man is that one can
ever and again become aware of the other as this being existing
over-against him, over against whom he himself exists. He
becomes aware of the other as one who relates to him out of his
selfhood and to whom he relates out of his selfhood. By virtue of
this characteristic reserved to him, man has not simply entered
into being as one species among other species—only just so much
more manifoldly endowed—but as a special sphere. For here, and
within what we call world only here, does the meeting of the one
with the other take place in full reality. Certainly there is nowhere
in all world-immanence a self-enclosed unity—this is as such
transcendence—but each individual is directed and referred to the
other. Only in man, however, does this interrelatedness transform
itself and issue into the reality of meeting in which the one exists
over against the other as his other, as one able in common
presence at once to withstand him and confirm him. Where this
self-being turned toward the partner over-against one is not lived,
the sphere of man is still unrealized. The human means the taking

place from one time to another of that meeting which is latent in the being of the world.

The insight that I have intimated here encounters ever again an impressive argument—only rarely, to be sure, in an outspoken manner, mostly as the wordless self-emphasis of "spiritual" persons. It is argued through a reference, mostly only just presented, to the alleged essential nature of mental work. This takes place not in a living over-against, ready for give and take, but in a fundamentally impermeable being-in-oneself that is alone accessible to the "spirit," that is, to ideas and images that emerge out of the all-encompassing depths of the self. The thinking of the thinker is said to bear the most unmistakable witness that this is so.

My experiences and observations have taught me to see it otherwise. Out of all the ages of man about whose spiritual work I know, I have become acquainted not merely with no great configuration, but also with no great thought whose origin was not to be gathered from the self-involving contact with existing being over-against one. The evolved substance which the spirit brings as a work into the ages has come to it out of the unreserved meetings of its personal bearers with otherness. For as in other respects there is in the world-immanence no self-enclosed unity, so also there is in it no self-enclosed unity of the spirit. Only through opening out, through entering into openness, does the spirit that has descended into the human realm win that coherence in work that has not already passed away in becoming. The fortress into which the self-possessed spirituality retreats before the exacting demand of answering life over against one is a gloriously painted coulisse.

It is the spirit that, having entered into the being of man, enables and fits him to live over-against in distance and relation; the spirit has thereby empowered man to be a special sphere of being. From this primal process has come forth the highest work-treasure of man, speech, the manifest proclamation of existing reciprocity between the one and the other. But the gifts of the spirit have also brought with them the great danger, becoming ever greater, that threatens mankind. It has belonged to the constitution of the human person as the bearer of the spirit that the basic situation of existing over-against also carries over here into the inwardness of the person. Thus there could develop a relationship of the individual to himself foreign to the non-human world, although here there naturally belonged to the situation of "being over-against" nothing of the structural difference and the independence of answer of being over-against in actual dialogue—unless it was in the case of a sickness that splits the personal coherence. But now at the same time the possibility opened that the dialogic of the soul cut itself off from all real communicating with the otherness outside it and degenerated into a self-enjoying of individual meaning, indeed to a hybris of an All-Self that arrogates to itself the self-enclosed unity of the Godhead existing before all creations and emanations. What was to be found as existing outside of the self was no longer the partner of a genuine reciprocity, but ultimately only the objective knots within a psyche that might certainly have been conceived in theory as more or less universal, but was lived as exclusively individual. By means of the universalizing philosophical positions, this individual self could be identified in practice simply with the Self and was no longer exposed to the claim of otherness.

My experience and observations have taught me to recognize in this degeneration the opponent of mankind, steadily increasing in might during the epochs of history, but especially in our time. It is none other than the spirit itself, cut off, that commits the sin against the holy spirit.

20. *Books and Men*

If I had been asked in my early youth whether I preferred to have dealings only with men or only with books, my answer would certainly have been in favor of books. In later years this has become less and less the case. Not that I have had so much better experiences with men than with books; on the contrary, purely delightful books even now come my way more often than purely delightful men. But the many bad experiences with men have nourished the meadow of my life as the noblest book could not do, and the good experiences have made the earth into a garden for me. On the other hand, no book does more than remove me into a paradise of great spirits, where my innermost heart never forgets I cannot dwell long, nor even wish that I could do so. For (I must say this straight out in order to be understood) my innermost heart loves the world more than it loves the spirit. I have not, indeed, cleaved to life in the world as I might have; in my relations with it I fail it again and again; again and again I remain guilty toward it for falling short of what it expects of me, and this is partly, to be sure, because I am so indebted to the spirit. I am indebted to the spirit as I am to myself, but I do not, strictly speaking, love it, even as I do not, strictly speaking, love myself. I do not in reality love him who has seized me with his heavenly clutch and holds me fast; rather I love her, the "world," who comes again and again to meet me and extends to me a pair of fingers.

Both have gifts to share. The former showers on me his manna of books; the latter extends to me the brown bread on whose crust I break my teeth, a bread of which I can never have enough: men. Aye, these tousle-heads and good-for-nothings, how I love them! I revere books—those that I really read—too much to be able to love them. But in the most venerable of living men I always find more to love than to revere: I find in him something of this world that is simply there as the spirit never can be there. The spirit hovers above me powerfully and pours out his exalted gift of speech, books; how glorious, how weird! But she, the human world, needs only to cast a wordless smile, and I cannot live without her. She is mute; all the prattle of men yields no word such as sounds forth constantly out of books. And I listen to it all in order to receive the silence that penetrates to me through it, the silence of the creature. But just the human creature! That creature means a mixture. Books are pure, men are mixed; books are spirit and word, pure spirit and purified word; men are made up of prattle and silence, and their silence is not that of animals but of men. Out of the human silence behind the prattle the spirit whispers to you, the spirit *as soul*. She, she is the beloved.

Here is an infallible test. Imagine yourself in a situation where you are alone, wholly alone on earth, and you are offered one of the two, books or men. I often hear men prizing their solitude but that is only because there are still men somewhere on earth even though in the far distance. I knew nothing of books when I came forth from the womb of my mother, and I shall die without books, with another human hand in my own. I do, indeed, close my door at times and surrender myself to a book, but only because I can open the door again and see a human being looking at me.

THE HEBREW UNIVERSITY
JERUSALEM, ISRAEL

61

Bibliography

1897

"Essays on Viennese Authors": Albenberg, Hofmannsthal, Schnitzler. (Polish) in *Przeglad tygodniowy*.

1899

Referat auf dem III. Zionistenkongress. St. Basel, August 15-18, 1899. Vienna: Verlag des Vereins "Erez Israel," p. 191 ff.

1900

"Ein Wort über Nietzsche und die Lebenswerte," *Kunst und Leben*, Berlin (December).

1901

"Kultur und Zivilisation," *Kunstwart*, Vol. 14, No. 15, 1. Maiheft.

Referat auf dem V. Zionisten-Kongress. Basel, December 26-30, 1901. Vienna: Verlag des Vereins "Erez Israel," pp. 151-170.

"Ueber Jakob Boehme," *Wiener Rundschau*, Vol. 5, No. 12 (June 15), pp. 251-253.

"Zwei nordische Frauen. (Ellen Key und Selma Lagerlöf)." *Neue Freie Presse* (Vienna), No. 13263 (July 20).

1903

(editor) *Der Jude; Revue der judischen Moderne*. Edited by Dr. Chaim Weizmann, Martin Buber, and Berthold Feiwel. Berlin: Jüdischer Verlag.

(editor) *Judische Kunstler*. Berlin: Jüdischer Verlag.

"Lesser Ury," *Judische Kunstler*. Ed. Martin Buber. Berlin: Jüdischer Verlag.

1904

"Gustav Landauer," *Die Zeit* (Vienna), Vol. 39, No. 506 (June 11).

"Zur Aufklärung," *Judische Rundschau*, Vol. 9, No. 48 (Dec. 2).

1905

"Die Duse in Florenz," *Die Schaubühne*, Vol. 1, No. 15 (Dec. 14).

"Uber jüdische Märchen," *Generalanzeiger für die gesamten Interessen des Judentums*, Berlin (August).

1906

"Drei Rollen Novellis," *Die Schaubuhne*, Vol. 2, No. 2 (Jan. 11).

"Einführung" (Introduction) to *Die Gesellschaft Sammlung sozial-psychologischer Monographien*, ed. Martin Buber. In Volume 1, Werner Sombart, *Das Proletariat*, Frankfurt am Main: Rütten & Loening.

Die Geschichten des Rabbi Nachman. Frankfurt am Main: Rütten & Loening.

"Die Geschichte von der Kräutertruhe und dem Kaiser zu Rom," *Die Welt,* Vienna, Vol. 10.

"Die Legende der Chassidim." No. 2, "Der Zukunfstbrief," *Die Welt* (Aug. 17).

"Die Neidgeborenen. Eine chassidische Legende," *Der Zeitgeist,* Beiblatt zum *Berliner Tageblatt* (Dec. 17).

1907

"Das Haus der Dämonen. Ein jüdisches Märchen," *Die Sonntagszeit,* Beilage zu No. 1547 der Wiener Tageszeitung *Die Zeit* (Jan. 13).

1908

Die Legende des Baalschem, Frankfurt am Main: Rütten & Loening.

1909

Ekstatische Konfessionen. Jena: Eugen Diedrichs Verlag.

"Das hohe Lied," *Die Welt,* Vol. 13, No. 14-15.

1910

"Lebte Jesus? Ein Brief an den Herausgeber," *Diskussion,* Kulturparlament, Vol. 1, No. 1.

1911

Chinesische Geister- und Liebesgeschichten. Frankfurt am Main: Rütten & Loening.

Drei Reden über das Judentum. Frankfurt am Main: Rütten & Loening.

"Mystik als religiöser Solipsismus. Bemerkungen zu einem Vortrag Ernst Troeltschs," *Verhandlungen des ersten deutschen Soziologentages 1910.* Tübingen: I. C. B. Mohr Verlag, pp. 206 ff.

1912

(editor) *Die Gesellschaft. Sammlung sozialpsychologischer Monographien.* 40 vols. Frankfurt am Main: Rütten & Loening, 1906-1912.

1913

Buberheft. Vol. 3, No. 1/2 of *Neue Blatter.* Hellerau/Berlin: Verlag der Neuen Blätter. Includes "Das Reden des Ekstatikers," "Von der Lehre," "Das verborgene Leben," "Das Judentum und die Menschheit," "Der Sinn der chassidischen Lehre," "Kultur und Religiosität," "Buddha," "Drei Legenden vom Baalschem," and Gustav Landauer, "Martin Buber."

Daniel. Gespräche von der Verwirklichung. Leipzig: Insel Verlag.

1914

"Bücher die jetzt und immer zu lesen sind." (Antwort auf eine Rundfrage), *Wiener Kunst- und Buchschau,* Vienna (December).

"Der Engel und die Weltherrschaft. Ein altjüdisches Märchen," *Jüdische Rundschau,* Berlin (Nov. 26).

Kalewala. (The national epic of Finland.) Translated by Anton Schiefner. Revised and supplemented with notes and introduction by Buber. Munich: Georg Müller.

Reden und Gleichnisse des Tschuang-Tse. Leipzig: Insel-Verlag.

(editor) *Die vier Zweige des Mabinogi.* Leipzig: Insel-Verlag.

1915

"Bewegung. Aus einem Brief an einen Höllander" (Frederik van Eeden), *Der Neue Merkur,* Munich (January-February).

"J. L. Perez," *Jüdischer National-Kalendar 5676.* Vienna: Verlag R. Löwit.

"Richtung soll kommen," *Masken,* Vol. 10, No. 11.

1916

Die jüdische Bewegung. Gesammelte Aufsätze und Ansprachen.

Vol. 1, 1900-1914. Berlin: Jüdischer Verlag. Includes "Jüdische Renaissance" (1900), "Gegenwartsarbeit" (1901), "Feste des Lebens" (1901), "Das Zion der jüdischen Frau" (1901), "Wege zum Zionismus" (1901), "Jüdische Wissenschaft" (1901), "Von jüdischer Kunst" (1902), "Die Schaffende, das Volk und die Bewegung" (1902), "Ein geistiges Zentrum" (1902), "Renaissance und Bewegung" 1. (1903), 2. (1910), "Zionistische Politik" (1904), "Was ist zu tun?" (1904), "Theodor Herzl" (1904), "Herzl und die Historie" (1904), "Die hebräische Sprache" (1910), "Das Land der Juden" (1912), "Er und Wir" (Herzl, 1910), "Das Gestaltende" (1912), "Zwiefache Zukunft" (1912), "Der Augenblick" (1914), "Die Tempelweihe" (1915), "Zum Gedächtnis" (1915).

Vom Geist des Judentums. Leipzig: Kurt Wolff Verlag.

(editor) *Der Jude; eine Monatsschrift.* Ed. Martin Buber. I-VIII. Berlin, R. Löwit (Jüdischer Verlag), 1916-1924.

"Von jüdischen Dichtern und Erzählern," *Jüdischer National-Kalendar, 5677.* Vienna: Verlag der Jüdischen Zeitung.

"Über Agnon" in *Treue, eine jüdische Sammelschrift,* edited by Leo Hermann. Berlin: Jüdischer Verlag.

1917

"Asketismus und Libertinismus," *Jüdische Rundschau,* Vol. 22, No. 42 (Oct. 19).

"Aus einem Rundschreiben vom Ostern 1914," *Almanach der neuen Jugend auf das Jahr 1917.* Berlin: Verlag der neuen Jugend.

Ereignisse und Begegnungen. Leipzig: Insel-Verlag. (Most of these essays were later included in *Hinweise* [1953].)

"Referat über jüdische Erziehung auf dem Deutschen Zionistichem Delegiertentag, December 1916," *Jüdische Rundschau,* Berlin (Jan. 5). See also "Eine Erklärung," *Jüdische Rundschau* (March 16).

"Sieben Geschichten vom Baalscham," *Judischer National-*

Kalender 5678. Vienna: Verlag "Jüdische Zeitung." (The sixth story, "Die Sabbatseele" was not included in *Die chassidischen Bucher* [1928].)

Völker, Staaten und Zion. Vienna: R. Löwit Verlag. (A letter to Hermann Cohen and comments on his reply. Later included in *Die Jüdische Bewegung*, Vol. II [1921].)

1918

"Brief über das Wesen der Sprache," der *Mitteilungen des Internationalenen Institutes für Philosophie in Amsterdam*, No. 1 (March). Groningen: Verlag P. Nordhoff.

Mein Weg zum Chassidismus. Erinnerungen. Frankfurt am Main: Rütten & Loening. (Later included in *Hinweise* [1953].)

"Rede bei der Tagung der jüdischen Jugendorganisationen Deutschlands am 5. März 1918," *Mitteilungen des Vergandes der jüdischen Jugendvereine Deutschlands*, Berlin, Heft 2/3 (April/May).

"Schreiben . . ." in *Mededeelingen van het International Instituut voor Wijsbegeerte te Amsterdam*: March. Letter to Mr. Borel published in Hebrew in *Mahut* (March 17, 1917).

1919

Cheruth. Eine Rede über Jugend und Religion. Vienna and Berlin: R. Löwit Verlag.

"Drei Geschichten von der Menschenliebe," *Der Jude*, Vol. 4, No. 9 (December).

Gemeinschaft, Vol. 2 of *Worte an die Zeit*. Munich: Dreiländer Verlag.

Grundsätze, Vol. 1, of *Worte an die Zeit*. Munich: Dreiländer Verlang.

Der Heilige Weg. Frankfurt am Main: Rütten & Loening.

"Landauer und die Revolution," *Masken, Halbmonatschrift des Düsseldorfer Schauspielhauses*, 14, No. 18/19 (1918/1919), pp. 282-286.

"Nicht was zum Munde eingeht," *Der Jude*, Vol. 4, No. 4 (July).

"Samael," *Der Jude*, Vol. 3, No. 12 (March).

"Die wahre Weisheit," *Der Jude*, Vol. 4, No. 4 (July).

"Zwei Tagebuchstellen. 1. Pescara an einem Augustmorgen (1914). 2. Nach der Heimkehr," *Zeit Echo. Ein Kriegstagebuch der Künstler*, Munich, No. 3.

"Die zweiten Tafeln (Moseslegende)," *Inselalmanach auf das Jahr 1919*. Leipzig: Insel-Verlag.

1920

"Der heimliche Führer (Ansprache über Landauer)," *Die Arbeit*, Berlin (June).

(editor) *Meister Eckharts mystische Schriften*, Gustav Landauer. Veränderte Neuausgabe. Berlin: Karl Schanbel Verlag.

Die Rede, die Lehre, und das Lied. Leipzig: Insel-Verlag. Includes introductory essays to *Ekstatische Konfessionen, Reden und Gleichnisse des Tschuang-Tse*, and *Kalewala*.

"Die Wanderschaft des Kinderlosen," Martin Buber, H. H. Cohn. Ch. Z. Klötzel, *Drei Legenden*, Berlin: Jüdischer Verlag.

1921

"Drei Predigten. 1. Das Weinen," *Gabe, Herrn Rabbiner Nobel zum 50. Geburtstag dargebracht*, Frankfurt am Main. (The second and third are included in *Die chassidischen Bücher* [1928].)

Die jüdische Bewegung. Gesammelte Aufsätze und Ansprachen. Vol. 2, 1916-1920. Berlin: Jüdischer Verlag. Includes "Die Lösung," "Argumente," "Mose," "Völker, Staaten und Zion: I. Begriffe und Wirklichkeit; II, Der Staat, und die Menschheit," "Der Wägende," "An die Prager Freunde," "Ein Heldenbuch," "Die Polnischen und Franz Blei," " 'Kulturarbeit'," "Unser Nationalismus," "Vorbemerkung über Franz Werfel," "Ein politischer Faktor," "Der Preis," "Die Eroberung Palästinas," "Jüdisch Leben," "Zion und die Jugend," "Eine unnötige Sorge," "Die Revolution und wir," "Vor der Entscheidung," "In später Stunde," "Anhang: Noten zu 'Völker, Staaten und Zion'."

"Rede über die politischen Prinzipien der Bewegung auf der 2. Hitachduth Konferenz, Karlsbad, August 1921" in the Yiddish weekly *Volk und Land* (Nov. 18 and 26).

(editor) *Der wederne Mensch* by Gustav Landauer. Potsdam: Gustav Kiepenheuer Verlag.

1922

"Die Aufgabe," *Das werdende Zeitalter*. Vol. 1, No. 2 (April).

"Drama und Theater," *Masken, Zeitschrift für deutsche Theaterkultur* (Düsseldorfer Schauspielhaus), Vol. 8, No. 1, pp. 5 ff. (Later included in *Hinweise* [1953].)

Der grosse Maggid und seine Nachfolge. Frankfurt am Main: Rütten & Loening.

"Über den deutschen Aufsatz," *Wilhelm Schneider; Meister des Stils über Sprache und Stillehre*. Leipzig: B. G. Teubner, 1922.

"Vier Gleichnisse des Ferid-ed-din-Attar," *Inselalmanach auf das Jahr 1922*.

1923

"Eine neue Lehre; zwei chassidische Schriftdeutungen," *Der Jude*, Vol. 7, No. 10/11 (January/February).

Ich und Du. Leipzig: Insel-Verlag.

Reden über das Judentum. Frankfurt am Main: Rütten & Loening. Includes *Drei Reden* (1911), the three talks from *Vom Geist des Judentums* (1916), *Der heilige Weg* (1918), and *Cheruth* (1919), plus an important Foreword.

"Religion und Gottesherrschaft, Besprechung von Leonhard Ragaz' *Weltreich, Religion und Gottesherrschaft*," Frankfurter Zeitung, "Literaturblatt," No. 9 (April 27).

Sette discorsi sull'ebraismo, Tradotti di Dante Lattes e Mosè Beilinson con una prefazione del Alessandro Bonucci, Firenze: Israel.

1924

(editor) *Beginnen*, Gustav Landauer. Köln: Marcan-Block-Verlag.

"Brief an Florens Christian Rang" in Florens Christian Rang *Deutsche Bauhütte*. Sannerz: Gemeinschaftsverlag Eberhard Arnold.

"Flucht?," Abendblatt der *Frankfurter Zeitung* (March 21). (Reply to Karl Wilker, *Frankfurter Zeitung* [March 6].)

"Geheimnis einer Einheit" in *Hermann Stehr, sein Werk und seine Welt*. Edited by Wihelm Meridies. Habelschwerdt: Franke Buchhandlung.

Das verborgene Licht. Frankfurt am Main: Rütten & Loening.

"Ein Wort über den Chassidismus," *Theologische Blatter* (Marburg), Vol. 3, Sp. 161.

1925

La leggenda del Baal-scem. Traduzione di Dante Lattes e Mosè Beilinson. Firenze: Israel.

"La Voie," translated by Bernard Poliakov. *La Revue juive* (Paris), Vol. 1, No. 6 (November). (Selections from *Reden über das Judentum*.)

"Zwiegespräch," *Insel-Almanach auf das Jahr 1926*. Leipzig: Insel-Verlag.

1926

"Gewalt und Liebe. Drei Verslein," *Das werdende Zeitalter*, Vol. 5, No. 1.

Die Kreatur, a quarterly. Ed. Martin Buber, Joseph Wittig, and Viktor von Weizsäcker. I-III. Berlin: L. Schneider, 1926-1930.

Rede über das Erzieherische. Berlin: Lambert Schneider Verlag.

"Résponse à un Questionnaire," *L'homme aprés la Mort*. Vol. 2 of *Les Cahiers Contemporains*. Editions Montaigne, Paris.

"Zwiegespräch (Kleine legendäre Anekdote nach dem Japanischen)," *Insel-Almanach auf das Jahr 1926*.

1927

Des Baal-Schemp-Tow Unterweisung im Umgang mit Gott.
Hellerau: Jakob Hegner Verlag.

"Schlichtung," *Frankfurter Zeitung*, 1. Morgenblatt (October 18,
1924). Reprinted in *Berliner Tageblatt*, Abendausgabe
(Feb. 26). (On Buddha-translation.)

1928

"Am Tag der Rückschau" (poem dedicated to P[aula] B[uber]).
Jüdische Rundschau, Berlin (Feb. 7).

Die chassidischen Bücher, Gesamtausgabe. Hellerau: Jakob
Hegner Verlag. Includes *Die Geschichten des Rabbi
Nachman, Die Legende des Baal-Schem, Mein Weg zum
Chassidismus, Der grosse Maggid und seine Nachfolge,* and
Das verborgene Licht.

"Drei Sätze eines religiösen Sozialismus," *Die Neue Wege*, 22,
pp. 327 ff. (Later included in *Hinweise* [1953].)

"Freiheit und Verantwortung," *Die Brücke*, Untermassfeld
(Dec. 24).

"Kraft und Richtung, Klugheit und Weisheit," *Das werdende
Zeitalter* (Kohlgrabe bei Vacha), Röhn (April).

"Natch dem Tod," *Munchener Neuesten Nachrichten* (February
8).

"Über die Todesstrafe," in E. M. Mungenast, *Der Mörder und
der Staat.* Stuttgart: Walter Hädecke Verlag, page 65.

"Über Rathenau (Briefliche Mitteilung)," in Harry Graf Kesler,
Walther Rathenau, sein Leben und sein Werk. Berlin-
Grünewald: Verlag Hermann Klemm, pp. 89 ff., n.

"Über Stefan George," *Literarische Welt*, Berlin (July 13).

"Zuchthaus für männliche Prostitution (Antwort auf eine Rundfrage)," *Das Forum*, Berlin (December).

1929

"Discours sur le judaïsme," Traduit de l'allemand par J.
Krichevsky. *L'Illustration juive*, Vol. 1, No. 2 (June 25).

(editor) *Gustav Landauer. Sein Lebensgang in Briefen.* Edited in cooperation with Ina Britschgi-Schimmer. 2 Vols. Frankfurt am Main: Rütten & Loening.

"Philosophie und Religiöse Weltanschauung in der Erwachsenenbildung" in *Tagungsbericht des Hohenrodter Bundes*, Vol. 2, Berlin.

"Reden auf der sozialistischen Tagung in Heppenheim: die Begründung des Sozialismus. Sozialismus und persönliche Lebensgestaltung" in *Sozialismus aus dem Glauben. Verhandlungen der sozialistischen Tagung in Heppenheim*, Pfingstwoche, 1928. Zürich: Rotapfel-Verlag, pp. 90 ff., 121 ff., 217 ff.

"Religion und Philosophie," *Europäische Revue* (August), pp. 325-335.

"Über Asien und Europa," *Chinesisch-deutscher Almanach für das Jahr 1929/1930.* Edited by China-Institute, Frankfurt am Main.

"Ein Wörterbuch der Hebräischen Philosophie. (Bespreschung von Jakob Klatzkins *Thesaurus philosophicus linguae hebraicae*)," *Frankfurter Zeitung, Literaturblatt* (Feb. 24).

1930

"Bemerkungen zu Jesaja," *Monatsschrift für Geschichte und Wissenschraft des Judentums*, Vol. 74, Nos. 5/6, 9/10 (May/June, September/October).

Hundert chassidische Geschichten. Berlin: Schocken Verlag.

1931

"Bemerkungen zur Gemeinschaftsidee," *Kommende Gemeinde*, Vol. 3, No. 2 (July). ("Was uns fehlt; Gedanken zum wirtschaflichen und sozialen Umbruch.")

"In jüngeren Jahren," in Harald Braun, *Dichterglaube. Stimmen religiösen Erlebens.* Berlin-Steglitz: Eckart.

Jewish Mysticism, and the Legends of the Baal-Schem. Translated by Lucy Cohen. Londen and Toronto: J. M. Dent

& Sons. Includes one story, "The New Year's Sermon," not included in the authorized translation of *The Legend of the Baal-Schem* by Maurice Friedman [(1955)].

"Religiöse Erziehung," *Das Werdende Zeitalter*, Vol. 10, No. 1 (January).

"Verflucht sei der Tag (Jeremia 20, 14-18)," *Der Morgen*, Vol. 6, No. 6 (February).

1932

"Haus Gottes: Stimmen über den Kunstbau der Zukunft" *Eckart*, Vol. 8, No. 10 (October).

Ich und Du. Reissued. Berlin: Schocken Verlag.

Königtum Gottes. Vol. 1 of *Das Kommende. Untersuchungen der Entstehungsgeschichte des messianischen Glaubens*. Berlin: Schocken Verlag.

"Meta-anthropological Crisis," *Transition*. The Hague: Servire.

Reden über das Judentum. Reissued. Berlin: Schocken Verlag.

Zwiesprache. Berlin: Schocken Verlag.

1933

"Adel" (Zum 60. Geburtstag von Leo Baeck), *Judische Rundschau*, Vol. 38, No. 41 (May 21).

"Gespräch um Gott; Bericht über zwei Meinungskämpfe," *Eckart*, Vol. 9, No. 2 (February).

"Le Judaïsme et L'Angoisse Mondiale," *La Revue juive de Geneve*, Vol. 1, No. 6 (March).

Kampf um Israel. Reden und Schriften (1921-1932). Berlin: Schocken Verlag. Includes "Vorrede," "Der dritte Tischfuss" (1926), "Das Judentum und die neue Weltfrage" (1930), "Der Glaube des Judentums" (1929), "Die Brennpunkte der jüdischen Seele," "Nachahmung Gottes" (1926), "Biblisches Führertum," "Weisheit und Tat der Frauen" (1929), " 'Pharisäertum' " (1925), "Bericht und

Berischtigung" (1926), "Vertrauen" (1926), "Achad-Haam-Gedenkrede in Berlin" (1927), "Achad-Hamm-Gedenkrede in Basel" (1927), "Zwei hebräische Bücher" (1928), "Der wahre Lehrer" (1923), "Der Acker und die Sterne" (1928), "Sache und Person" (1929), "Die Tränen" (1928), "Philon und Cohen" (1928), "Für die Sache der Treue" (1930), "Franz Rosenzweig" (1930), "Der Dichter und die Nation" (1922), "Alfred Mombert" (1922), "Ein Wort über Franz Kafka" (1928), "Greif nach der Welt, Habima!" (1929), "Im Anfang" (1927), "Drei Stationen" (1929), "Nationalismus," "Lebensfrömmigkeit" (1928), "Zion und die Gola" (1932), "Wie kann Gemeinschaft werden?" (1930), "Arbeitsglaube" (1929), "Warum muss der Aufbau Palästinas ein sozialistischer sein?" (1929), "Universität und Volkschochschule," "Volkserziehung als unsere Aufgabe" (1926), "Rede auf dem XIII. Zionistenkongress in Karlsbad" (1922), "Kongressnotizen zur zionistischen Politik" (1921), "Zur Klärung" (1922), "Streiflichter" (1922), "Nachbemerkung" (1922), "Frage und Antwort" (1922), "Die Vertretung" (1923), "Selbstbesinnung" (1926), "Brief an das Aktions-Comité der Zionistischen Weltorganisation" (1928), "Rede auf dem XVI. Zionistenkongress in Basel" (1930), "Jüdisches Nationalheim und nationale Politik in Palästina," "Wann denn?" (1932).

"Name verpflichtet," *Kulturbund Deutscher Juden Monatsblätter*, Vol. 1, No. 1 (October).

"Die Söhne," *Die Logen-Schwester*, Vol. 6, No. 11 (Nov. 15).

Die Tröstung Israels; aus Jeschajahu, Kapitel 40 bis 55. Mit der Verseutschung von M. B. und Franz Rosenzweig. Berlin: Schocken-Bücherei des Schocken-Verlags, 1.

"Zur Ethik der politischen Entscheidung," *Politik und Ethik.* Petzen: Versöhnungsbund.

1934

Erzählungen von Engeln, Geistern und Dämonen. Berlin: Schocken Verlag.

"Jiskor; Einleitung zu einem Gedenkbuch," *Jisrael Volk und Land; jüdische Anthologie.* Berlin: Hechaluz, Deutscher Landesverband.

"Die Tugend der Propaganda," *Jüdische Rundschau*, Vol. 39, No. 43 (May 29).

"Über Selbstmord: Antwort auf eine Rundfrage" in Karl Baumann, *Selbst-Mord und Freitod in sprachlicher und geistesgeschichtlicher Beleuchtung* (Diss. Giessen, 1933), Würzburg-Aumühle: K. Trilsch.

1935

Deutung des Chassidismus. Berlin: Schocken Verlag. (Later included in *Die chassidische Botschaft.*)

Martin Buber. ("The Meaning," "Of Oneness," "Ultimate Aims," "The True Foundation," "The Central Myth," "The Only Way," "The Primal Powers") in Ludwig Lewisohn, *Rebirth; a Book of Modern Jewish Thought.* New York: Harper.

"Vorbemerkung" to Hermann Cohen, *Der Nächste.* Berlin: Schocken Verlag.

1936

"Auf den Ruf hören: Schlusswort im Gespräch Martin Buber-Joachim Prinz," *Israelitisches Familienblatt*, Vol. 38, No. 33 (Aug. 13).

Aus Tiefen rufe ich Dich; dreiundzwanzig Psalmen in der Urschrift mit der Verdeutschung von M. B. Berlin: Schocken, = Bücherei des Schocken-Verlags, 51.

"Die Bibel als Erzähler; Leitwortstil in der Pentateuch-Erzählung," *Morgen*, Vol. 11, Nos. 11, 12 (February, March).

"Erkenntnis tut not," *Almanach des Schocken Verlags auf das Jahr 5696* (1935/36), pp. 11-14. Berlin: Schocken Verlag.

Die Frage an den Einzelnen. Berlin: Schocken Verlag.

"Geneisisprobleme," *Monatsschrift fur Geschichte und Wissenschaft des Judentums* (April 3).

Königtum Gottes. 2nd enlarged edition. Berlin: Schocken Verlag.

"Die Nacht der Gola; drei Midraschim," Translated by Martin Buber, *Almanach des Schocken Verlags auf das Jahr 5697.* Berlin: Schocken Verlag.

(with Franz Rosenzweig) *Die Schrift und ihre Verdeutschung.* Berlin: Schocken Verlag.

Die Stunde und die Erkenntnis. Reden und Aufsätze, 1933-1935. Berlin: Schocken Verlag. Includes "Der jüdische Mensch von heute," "Das Erste," "Die Kinder," "Gericht und Erneuerung," "Geschehende Geschichte," "Freiheit und Aufgabe," "Der Jude in der Welt," "Das Haltende," "Worauf es ankommt," "Ein Spruch des Maimuni," "Erkenntnis tut not," "Die Lehre und die Tat," "Die Mächtigkeit des Geistes," "Unser Bildungsziel," "Biblischer Humanismus," "Aufgaben jüdischer Volserziehung," "Jüdische Erwachsenenbildung," "Bildung und Weltanschauung," "Entwürfe und Programme," "Kirche, Staat, Volk, Judentum," "Brief an Ernest Michel," "Offener Brief an Gerhard Kittel," "Zu Gerhard Kittels 'Antwort'."

Zion als Ziel und Aufgabe. Berlin: Schocken Verlag.

"Zum Einheitscharakter des Jesajabuches," *Der Morgen*, Vol. 12, No. 8 (November).

1937

"Der Chaluz und seine Welt (Aus einer Rede)" *Almanach des Schocken Verlag auf das Jahr 5697* (1936/37), pp. 87-92. Berlin: Schocken Verlag.

"Dialogues," Traduit de l'allemand par Germain Landier Includes Réminiscences. La communion dans le silence. La profondeur inexprimable. De penser. *Mesures*, 4 (Oct. 15).

"Gespräche um Gott; Bericht über zwei Meinungskäampfe," *Almanach des Schocken Verlags auf das Jahr 5698*. Berlin: Schocken Verlag.

I and Thou. Translation of *Ich und Du* by Ronald Gregor Smith. Edinburgh: T. & T. Clark.

"Offenbarung und Gesetz" (from letters to Franz Rosenzweig), *Almanach des Schocken Verlags auf das Jahr 5697 (1936/37)*, pp. 147-154.

Die Schrift. Translation of the Bible from Hebrew into German in cooperation with Franz Rosenzweig. 15 vols. Berlin: Lambert Schneider and later Schocken Verlag. I. Im Anfang. (1926?). II. Namen. (1926). III. Er rief. (1926). IV. In der Wüste. (1927). VI. Jehoschua. (1927). VII. Richter. (1927). VIII. Schamuel. (1928). IX. Könige. (1929). X. Jeschajahu. (1930). XI. Jimejahu. (1931). XII. Jecheskel. (1932). XIII. Das Buch der Zwölf. (1934). XIV. Das Buch der Preisungen. (1935). XV. Gleichsprüche. (1937?).

1938

"Die Erwählung Israels; eine Befragung der Bibel," in *Almanach des Schocken Verlags auf das Jahr 5699*. Berlin: Schocken.

Die Forderung des Geistes und die geschichtliche Wirklichkeit; Antrittsvorlesung gehalten am 25. April 1938 in der Hebraischen Universität, Jerusalem. Leipzig: Schocken.

"Gegen die Untreue," *Jüdische Rundschau*, Vol. 43, No. 59 (July 26).

Je et Tu. Translated (from *Ich und Du*) by Geneviève Bianquis. Preface by Gaston Bachelard. Paris: Fernand Aubier, Editions Montaigne.

"Keep Faith," *The Palestine Post* (July 18).

Martin Buber und sein Werk. Zu seinem sechzigsten Geburtstag im Februar 1938 überreicht vom Schocken Verlag—Jüdischer Buchverlag. Berlin: Schocken.

"Chassidismus"; "Dienst an Israel"; "An das gleichzeitig"; "Die Biberlarbeit."

"Mitoldot hasheilah 'ma hu haadam'?" (in Hebrew). *Turim* (June 29).

"Ruach Israel bifney hameziut hanochchit" (in Hebrew). *Haaretz* (Dec. 30).

"Tviaat Haruach vehameziut Hahistorit" (in Hebrew). *Harzaat Peticha.* Jerusalem: The Hebrew University.

"Tviaat Haruach vehameziut hanochchit" (in Hebrew). *Mosnayim*, No. 7, Iyyar.

"Die Verwirklichung des Menschen: zur Anthropologie Martin Heideggers" in *Philosofia*, edited by Arthur Liebert, Vol. 3, No. 1-4, Belgrade.

"Wahrt die Treue," *Tirgumim*, Vol. 2, No. 310 (July 26).

Worte an die Jugend (I. Was ist zu tun? II. Zion und die Jugend. III. Cherut. IV. Wie kann Gemeinschaft werden. V. Warum soll man lernen? VI. Wann denn? VII. Vorurteile der Jugend). Berlin: Schocken,-Bücherei des Schocken-Verlags, 88.

1939

"Betichut heatid haenoschi ezel Hegel ve Marx," *Davar* (Jan. 20).

"Das Ende der deutsch-jüdischen Symbiose," *Jüdische Welt-Rundschau*, Vol. 1, No. 1 (March 10).

"Nationale Erziehung," Cernauti: Verlag des "Morgenblatt."

"Pseudo-Simsonismus," in *Jüdische Welt-Rundschau*, Vol. 1, No. 15 (June 23).

(with Judah Magnes) *Two Letters to Gandhi.* (Public letters by Buber and Magnes and the original text of Gandhi's statement about the Jews in *Harijan*, Nov. 26, 1938.) Pamphlets of *The Bond.* Jerusalem: Rubin Mass, April 1939.

"Zur Erzählung von Abraham." *Monatsschrift für Geschichte und Wissenschaft des Judentums*, Vol. 83, (January/ December).

"Zwei Beiträge zur Klärung des Pazifismus; Botschaft Dr. M. B.s an den Schulungskurs der Internat. Friedens-Akademie, Schloss Greng, 1.-12. August 1939," *Der Aufbau*, Vol. 20, No. 37 (Sept. 15).

1940

"Het Geloof van Israel." Translated by L. Alons, in Gerhardus van der Leeuw, *De godsdiensten der wereld*. I. Amsterdam: H. Meulenhoff.

"Neviei Sheker" (in Hebrew), *Lamoed*. Jerusalem.

"Reishitah shel hahassidut" (in Hebrew), *Jahadut Polin*, Tevet and Adar Alef, Jerusalem; also in *Mosnayim*, No. 11, Tamuz and Av.

"Tirgum Hamikra, Kavanato vedrahav" (in Hebrew), *Mosnayim*, No. 10, Kislev/Tev. 5700.

1941

" 'Defaitismus'; zu einer Diskussion," *Mitteilungsblatt der Hitachduth Olej Germania we Olej Austria*, Vol. 5, No. 50 (Dec. 12).

"Elohei Israel veilohei Avot" (in Hebrew), *Zion*, No. 7.

Gog und Magog (in Hebrew), *Davar*, serially (Oct. 23-Jan 10).

"Goyim veeilohav" (in Hebrew), *Kenesset*, Comments of Israeli writers on Bialik, ed. Jakov Cohen. Tel Aviv: Dvir Publishing Co.

"Humaniut Ivrit" (in Hebrew), *Hapoel Hazir*, No. 34 (May 30).

"Sheilat Doro shel Iyov" (in Hebrew), *Mosnayim*, No. 13, Tishri-Heshvan 5702.

1942

"Am umanhig" (in Hebrew), *Mosnayim*, Iyyar 5702.

"Baayat haadam bemishnato shel Heidegger" (in Hebrew), *Sdarim*, Collection of essays by writers of Israel, ed. A. Steimann. Tel Aviv.

"Behamulat hasan'gorim" (in Hebrew), *Mosnayim*, No. 15, Tishri.

"Darkei Hadat bearzeinu (Emet Veemunah)" (in Hebrew), *Machbarot lesifrut*, No. 2 (May).

"Hayesh Koach laruach? Le Mishnatoh shel Max Scheler" (in Hebrew), *Machbarot lesifrut*, No. 1 (September).

"Hayessod hautopi besozialism" (in Hebrew), *Hapoel Hazaïr*, No. 6 (December 24).

"Haruach vehameziut" (in Hebrew), *Machbarot lesifrut*, Tel Aviv.

"Lao-Tse al hashilton" (in Hebrew), *Hapoel Hazaïr*, No. 35 (May 20).

"Lehinui 'Hasozialism hautopisti' " (in Hebrew), *Hapoel Hazaïr*, No. 36 (Nov. 30).

"Raayon hageulah behassidut" (in Hebrew), *Arahim*, Jerusalem: Reuben Mass, Library for Institute for Leaders.

Torat haneviim. Jerusalem: Mosad Bialik.

1943

"Baayat haadam" (in Hebrew), *Machbarot lesifrut*, Tel Aviv.

"Dat uphilosophia" (in Hebrew), *Hagot*, Jerusalem: The Philosophical Society (Hugo Bergmann's 60th Birthday).

"In Theresienstadt," *Mitteilungsblatt*, Vol. 7, No. 21 (May 21).

"Israel bearzo besefer 'Kusari' " (in Hebrew), *Gilyonot*, Nos. 14 & 10, Shevat & Adar A (from *Bein Am learzo*).

"Kropotkin" (in Hebrew), *Hapoel Hazaïr*, June 7.

"Al mahutah shel Hatarbut" (in Hebrew), *Machbarot lesifrut*, No. 2 (November).

"Pirutav shel Raajon" (in Hebrew), (tekes Hajovel letorat Copernicus, The Hebrew University Jerusalem), *Haaretz* (June 4).

"Proudhon" (in Hebrew) in *Hapoel Hazaïr* (April 29).

"Zadik ba laaretz (Nachmann mi Bratzlav)" (in Hebrew), *Mosnayim*, No. 17. Tishri.

1944

"Advice to frequenters of libraries," "Books for your vacation."
Branch Library book news, The New York Public Library,
Vol. 21, No. 5 (May).

"Ahavat Elohim veideot haelohut" (al Hermann Cohen) (in
Hebrew), *Knesset*, Vol. 8, Tel Aviv: Dvir Co.

"An Chaim Weizmann," *Mitteilungsblatt*, Vol. 8, No. 48 (Dec.
1).

"Bergson vehaintuiziah" (in Hebrew), Introduction in Part I of
Henri Bergson: Energiah Ruchanit (Hebrew translation of
Bergson's *Creative Evolution*), Tel Aviv: "L'guulam"
(Mosad Bialik).

"Dat umussar behassidut (Bepardeis Hahassidut)" (in Hebrew),
Amundim, Nos. 1, 9 & 10 (Sept. 15, 20).

"Leinjan *Gog u Magog*" (in Hebrew), *Haaretz* (Dec. 8).

"Lekach Mi-Sin" (in Hebrew), *Hagalgal*, No. 1 (Jan. 20).

"Mekomo shel Copernicus bephilosophia" in *Nicolai Copernicus*
by Sh. Smebasky (lectures at The Hebrew University, May
26). Jerusalem: The Hebrew Press.

"Marx, Lenin vehithadshut hahevra" (in Hebrew), *Mosnayim*,
No. 18, Nisan.

"Social experiments in Jewish Palestine," *The New Palestine*,
Vol. 35, No. 1 (Oct. 13).

"Spinoza veha Baal-Shem-Tov" (in Hebrew), *Machborot
lesifrut*, Nos. 3 & 2 (December) (from *Beparades
hahassidut*).

1945

Bfardes hachasidut (in Hebrew), Tel Aviv: Mosad Bialik through
Dvir.

Bein Am learzo (in Hebrew), Jerusalem: Schocken.

"The Crisis and the Truth; a Message," *The Australian Jewish
Review*, Vol. 6, No. 7 (September).

Darko shel Adam (meolam hahassidut) (in Hebrew), Jerusalem:
Hagalgal and also Mosad Bialik.

"Eternal truths," *The Zionist Record* (New Year annual) November.

For the Sake of Heaven. Translated from the German by Ludwig Lewisohn. Philadelphia: The Jewish Publication Society (Trans. of *Gog und Magog*) (1949).

"Judah Halevi's *Kitab al Kusari*," *Contemporary Jewish Record*, Vol. 8, No. 3 (June).

Le Message Hassidique. Translated by Phillipe Lavastine (extracts from *Die chassidischen Bücher*). In *Dieu Vivant*, 2.

Moshe (in Hebrew), Jerusalem: Schocken.

"Our Reply," in *Towards Union in Palestine, Essays on Zionism and Jewish-Arab Cooperation.* ed. Martin Buber, Judah L. Magnes, and Ernst Simon. Jerusalem: Ihud Association, pp. 33-36.

"The Philosophical Anthropology of Max Scheler." Translated from the German by Ronald Gregor Smith. *Philosophy and Phenomenological Research*, Vol. 6, No. 2 (December).

"To Chaim Weizmann," in *Chaim Weizmann; a Tribute on His Seventieth Birthday*, ed. Paul Goodman. London: V. Gollancz.

"The Beginning of the National Ideal," *Review of Religion*, X (1945-1946), pp. 254-265.

De Legende van den Baalsjém. Translated by R(eine) Colacço Osorio-Swaab. -Deventer, Kluwer.

"The Education of Character" (an address to the National Conference of Palestinian teachers at Tel Aviv in May 1939). Translated from the German by Ronald Gregor Smith, in *The Mint; a miscellany*, (ed. Geoffrey Grigson), London: Routledge.

"God's Word and Man's Interpretation," *The Palestine Post* (April 8).

Introduction in *Chinese Ghost and Love Stores* (a selection from the Liao Chai stories by P'u Sung-Ling, trans. Rose Quong). New York: Pantheon.

Mamre. Essays in Religion. Translated by Greta Hort.

Melbourne and London: Melbourne University Press & Oxford University Press. All but one of these essays have later been republished in new, authorized translations.

Moses. Oxford: East West Library.

"Der Ort des Chassidismus in der Religionsgeschichte," *Theologische Zeitschrift II*, 6 (November/December).

Palestine, a bi-national state (M. B., Judah L. Magnes, Moses Smilansky). New York: Ihud. Public hearings before the Anglo-American Committee of Inquiry. Jerusalem (Palestine), March 14, 1946.

"Ragaz veisrael" (in Hebrew), *Baayot*, No. 3 (February).

1947

Arab-Jewish Unity. Testimony before the Anglo-American Inquiry Commission for the Ihud (Union) Association by Judah Magnes and Martin Buber. London: Victor Gollancz Ltd.

Between Man and Man. Translated by Ronald Gregor Smith. London: Kegan Paul, 1947). Includes "Dialogue," "The Question to the Single One," "Education," "The Education of Character," and "What Is Man?"

Dialogisches Leben. Gesammelte philosophische und pädagogische Schriften. Zürich: Gregor Müller Verlag. Includes *Ich und Du, Zwiesprache, Die Frage an den Einzelnen, Über das Erzieherische*, "Über Charaktererziehung," *Das Problem des Menschen*.

"Emunah ba-ruach" (in Hebrew), *Haaretz* (Oct. 31).

Der Knecht Gottes; Schicksal, Aufgabe, Trost. The songs of the servant of the Lord from Jeremiah and Isaiah in the Buber-Rosenzweig translation with introduction and commentary by Henri Friedlaender.- 's Gravenhage: Pulvis Viarum.

Martin Buber, zijn leven en zijn werk; verzameld en bewerkt door Juliette Binger. Ingeleid door W. Banning. -'s Graveland: De Driehoek.

Netivot beutopia (in Hebrew), Tel Aviv: Am Oved. Also in Library of Knowledge.

"Ragaz und 'Israel' " (Address at a memorial for Ragaz in the synagogue Emet Ve-Emuna, Jerusalem), *Neue Wege*, XLI, 11 (November).

Tales of the Hasidim, The Early Masters. Translated by Olga Marx. New York: Schocken Books.

Ten Rungs, Hasidic Sayings. Translated by Olga Marx. New York: Schocken Books.

1948

Chinesische Geister- und Liebesgeschichten. Reissued as a volume in the Manesse Bibliothek der Weltliteratur. Zürich: Manesse Verlag.

Hasidism. New York: The Philosophical Library. (All these essays have been retranslated in the authorized translations by Maurice Friedman in *Hasidism and Modern Man* [1958] & *Origin & Meaning of Hasidism* [1960].)

Israel and the World. Essays in a Time of Crisis. New York: Schocken Books. Includes "The Faith of Judaism," "The Two Foci of the Jewish Soul," "The Prejudices of Youth," "The Love of God and the Idea of Deity," "Imitation Dei," "In the Midst of History," "What Are We To Do about the Ten Commandments?," "The Man of Today and the Jewish Bible," "Plato and Isaiah," "False Prophets," "Biblical Leadership," "Teaching and Deed," "Why We Should Study Jewish Sources," "On National Education," "The Jew in the World," "The Power of the Spirit," "The Spirit of Israel and the World of Today," "The Gods of the Nations and God," "Nationalism," "The Land and its Possessors," " 'And If Not Now, When?'," "Hebrew Humanism."

Moses. Zürich: Gregor Müller.

"November," *Mitteilungsblatt*, Vol. 12, No. 44 (November 5).

Das Problem des Menschen. Heidelberg: Verlag Lambert Schneider.

Tales of the Hasidim, The Later Masters. Translated by Olga Marx. New York: Schocken Books.

Der Weg des Menschen, Nach der chassidischen Lehre. Jerusalem: copyright by Martin Buber. Published in the Netherlands by "Pulvis Viarum" Press.

"Zweierlei Zionismus," *Die Stunde; einmalige Ausgabe.* Jerusalem (May 28).

1949

"Al hayessod hahinuchi" (in Hebrew), *Sefer Dinaburg*, collected essays (ed. Isaac Baar, Joshua Gutman, & Moshe Shova), Jerusalem: Kiryat Sefer. (Translation of *Erziehung*.)

"Ein Briefwechsel" (by Karl Thieme) with M. B. in *Rundbrief zur Förderung der Freundschaft zwischen dem alten und dem neuen Gottesvolk—im Geiste der beiden Testamente*, Vol. 2, No. 5/6 (December).

"Eine Erwiderung," *Neue Wege,* Vol. 43, No. 9 (November).

"Erwachsenenbildung" in *Festschrift der Nueva Communidad Israelita, 5700-5710*. Buenos Aires.

Gog und Magog. Eine Chronik, Heidelberg: Verlag Lambert Schneider.

(Interview). (M. Benson: Jérusalem en trêve), *Cahiers sioniens*, Vol. 3, No. 5 (Jan. 1).

"Let us make an end to falsities," *Freeland*, Vol. 5, No. 1 (January/February).

Paths in Utopia. Translated by R. F. C. Hull. London: Routledge & Kegan Paul.

The Prophetic Faith. Translated from the Hebrew by Carlyle Witton-Davies. New York: The Macmillan Co.

"Vorwort" in Jacob Burckhardt, *Tarbut Harenaissance beitaliah*.

"Zur Situation der Philosophie," *Library of the Xth International Congress of Philosophy* (Amsterdam, Aug. 11-18, 1948), Vol. I: *Proceedings of the Congress*, p. 317 ff.

1950

"Bnei Amos" (in Hebrew), *Ner*, No. 1 (April 29).

"Hinuch Mevugarim" (in Hebrew), *Molad*, No. 4, 24/23, Shevat-Adar.

"Hinuch uvehinat Olam" (in Hebrew), *Orot*, ed. by Abraham Levinson. Tel-Aviv: Histadrut haklalit shel haovdim haivriim beeretz Israel.

Die Erzählungen der Chassidim. Manesse-Bibliothek der Weltliteratur. Zürich: Manesse-Verlag.

"Les Dieux des peuples et Dieu; de l'idée nationale chez Krochmal et Dostoïewsky," *Revue de la Pensée juive*, 3 (April).

Der Glaube der Propheten. Zürich: Manesse Verlag.

"Gvurat Haruach" (in Hebrew), *Davar*, 25th Jubilee issue.

Hazedek vehaavel al pi Zror mismorei tehillim (in Hebrew). Jerusalem: Magnes Press.

Interview, in *Rundbrief zur Förderung der Freundschaft zwischen dem alten und dem neuen Gottesvolk—im Geiste der beiden Testament* II, 7 (April).

Israel und Palästina. Zur Geschichte einer Idee. Erasmus Bibliothek, edited by Walter Rüegg. Zürich: Artemis-Verlag.

"Jesus und der Knecht," in *Pro regno, pro sanctuario; een bundel studies en bijdragen van vrienden en vereerders bij de zestigste* verjaardag van Prof. Dr. G. van der Leeuw . . . onder redactie van W. J. Kooiman en J. M. van Veen. Nijkerk, G. F. Callenbach.

"Maase hamlahat Shaul" (in Hebrew), *Tarbiz*, No. 22, Tishri-Tevet.

"Myth in Judaism." Translated by Ralph Manheim. *Commentary*, Vol. 9 (June), pp. 562-566.

"A New Venture in Adult Education," *The Hebrew University of Jerusalem*. Semi-jubilee volume published by The Hebrew University, Jerusalem (April), pp. 116-120.

Pfade in Utopie. Heidelberg: Verlag Lambert Schneider.

"Remarks on Goethe's Concept of Humanity," *Goethe and the Modern Age* (ed. Arnold Bergstraesser). Chicago: Henry Regnery, pp. 227-233. (Later included in *Pointing the Way* [1957].)

"A Talk with Tagore" in *India and Israel*, Vol. 3, Nos. 4/5 (October/November).

Torat Haneviim (in Hebrew), second edition. Jerusalem: Mosad Bialik.

"Über den Kontakt." Aus Jerusalemer pädagogischen Radio-Reden, in *Die Idee einer Schule im Spiegel der Zeit; Festschrift für Paul Geheeb zum 80. Geburtstag und zum 40 jährigen Bestehen der Odenwaldschule.* Heidelberg: L. Schneider.

The Way of Man, according to the Teachings of Hasidism. London: Routledge & Kegan Paul; Chicago: Wilcox & Follett. (Reprinted in *Hasidism and Modern Man* [1958, Book IV].)

"Zikron Pegishah" (A Talk with Tagore) (in Hebrew), *Ner* (Sept. 27).

1951

Bücher und Menschen. A four-page booklet privately printed and not sold to the public. St. Gallen: Tschudy-Verlag. Also in *Hinweise* (1953).

"Distance and Relation." Translated by Ronald Gregor Smith. *The Hibbert Journal* (January), Vol. 49, pp. 105-113.

"Hadussiah bein haelohim vehaadam bamikra" (in Hebrew), *Megilot*, No. 6, Av. (Lecture given in French in November 1950 in Paris for the convention for education of European, African, and Australian countries.)

"Heilung aus der Begegnung," *Neue Schweizer Rundschau*, Vol. 19, No. 6 (October).

"Individual and society," in Stanley R. Brav, *Marriage and the Jewish Tradition; toward a Modern Philosophy of Family Living.* New York, The Philosophical Library.

"Judaism and civilization," in *The Present Contribution of Judaism to Civilization* (report of the seventh international and twenty-fifth anniversary Conference [July 12 to July 18.] London, The World Union for Progressive Judaism.

"Nachtrag zu einem Gespräch," *Die Neue Zeitung* (Feb. 21).

"Die Opferung Isaaks," *Frankfurter Hefte*, Vol. 6, No. 9 (September).

"Society and the State," *World Review* New Series 27 (May), pp. 5-12. Also in *Pointing the Way* (1957).

Zwei Glaubensweisen, Zürich: Manesse Verlag, 1950.

Two Types of Faith. Translated by Norman P. Goldhawk. London: Routledge & Kegan Paul; New York: The Macmillan Co., 1952; Harper Torchbooks (paperback), 1961.

Urdistanz und Beziehung. Heidelberg: Verlag Lambert Schneider. (Also published in *Studia Philosophica*, Jahrbuch der Schweizerischen philosophischen Gesellschaft. Vol. 10 [1950], pp. 7-19.)

"Zum Probelm der "Gesinnungsgemeinschaft," in *Robert Weltsch zum 60. Geburtstag; ein Gluckwunsch gewidmet von Freuden*. Tel Aviv—Jerusalem, Privatdruck.

1952

"Abstrakt und Konkret" (additional note to "Hoffnung für diese Stunde" [1952],) *Neue Schweizer Rundschau*, Vol. 20, No. 8 (December), *Merkur*, Vol. 7, No. 1 (January). (Also in *Hinweise* ([1953]).

"Adult Education," *Torah* (Magazine of Natl. Federation of Jewish Men's Clubs of United Synagogue of America), June.

An der Wende. Feden über das Judentum. Köln and Olten: Jakob Hegner Verlag.

At the Turning. Three Addresses on Judaism. New York: Farrar, Straus & Young.

"Bekenntnis des Schriftstellers," *Neue Schweizer Rundschau* N. F. XX, 3 (July) (Zum 75. Geburtstag von Hermann Hesse, 2. July).

Bilder von Gut und Böse. Kön und Olten: Jakob Hegner Verlag.

Die chassidische Botschaft. Heidelberg: Verlag Lambert Schneider. Includes "Spinoza, Sabbatai Zwi und der Baalschem" (1927), "Die Anfänge" (1943), "Der Grundstein" (1943), "Geist und Leib der Bewegung" (1921), "Sinnbildliche und Sakramentale Existenz" (1934), "Gott und die Seele" (1943), "Gottesliebe und Nächstenliebe" (1934), "Der Ort des Chassidismus in der Religionsgeschichte" (1943). The last essay centers on a comparison between Hasidism and Zen Buddhism.

Eclipse of God. Studies in the Relation between Religion and Philosophy. Translated by Maurice Friedman, et al. New York: Harper & Brothers. London: Gollancz, 1953. Includes "Report on Two Talks," "Religion and Reality," "Religion and Philosophy" (revised), "The Love of God and the Idea of Deity," "Religion and Modern Thinking," "Religion and Ethics," "On the Suspension of the Ethical," "God and the Spirit of Man," "Supplement: Reply to C. G. Jung."

"Erwiderung an C. G. Jung," *Merkue Deutsche Zeitschrift für europaisches Denken*, Vol. 6, No. 5 (May).

"Heilung aus der Begegnung," Preface to Hans Trüb, *Heilung aus der Begegnung. Eine Auseinandersetzung mit der Psychologie C. G. Jungs*. (Ed. Ernst Michel and Arie Sborowitz). Stuttgart: Ernst Klett Verlag.

"Hoffnung für diese Stunde," *Merkur*, Vol. 6, No. 8 (August); *Neue Schweizer Rundschau*, Vol. 20, No. 5 (September), pp. 270-278. Also in *Hinweise* (1953).

"Hope for This Hour." Translated by Maurice Friedman. Address given in English at Carnegie Hall, New York City, April 6. *World Review*, December. (Also in *Pointing the Way* [1957].)

Images of Good and Evil. Translated by Michael Bullock. London: Routledge & Kegan Paul.

Israel and Palestine. The History of an Idea. Translated by Stanley Godman. London: East and West Library; New York: Farrar, Straus & Young.

Moses. Heidelberg: Verlag Lambert Schneider.

"On the Suspension of the Ethical." Translated by Maurice Friedman. *Moral Principles of Action,* ed. Ruth Nanda Anshen, Vol. VI of Science of Culture Series. New York: Harper & Brothers. (Also in *Eclipse of God* [1952].)

Recht und Unrecht. Deutung einiger Psalmen. Basel: Sammlung Klosterberg, Verlag B. Schwabe.

"Religion und modernes Denken," *Merkur,* Vol. 6, No. 2 (February), pp. 101-120. (Also in *Gottesfinsternis* [1953].)

Right and Wrong. An Interpretation of Some Psalms. Translated by Ronald Gregor Smith. London: S.C.M. Press Ltd. (Also in *Good and Evil* [1953].)

"Le Sacrifice d'Isaac." Traduit de l'allemand par Claire Champollion. *Dieu vivant* 22.

Zwischen Gesellschaft und Staat. Heidelberg: Verlag Lambert Schneider.

1953

(Auswahl deutscher Verse), in Georg Gerster, *Trunken von Gedichten; eine Anthologie geliebter deutscher Verse, ausgewählt und kommentiert von . . .* M.B. (*u.a.*) . . . Zürich: Verlag der Arche. (Goethe, Hölderlin, Hoffmannsthal).

Das echte Gespräch und die Möglichkeiten des Friedens. Speech made by Buber on occasion of receiving the Friedenspreis des Deutschen Buchhandels, Frankfurt am Main, Paulskirche, September 17. Heidelberg: Lambert Schneider Verlag. Also found as part of *Martin Buber, Friedenspreis des Deutschen Buchhandels,* pp. 33-41, and in *Hinweise.*

"The Cultural Role of the Hebrew University." Translated by David Sidorsky. *The Reconstructionist,* Vol. 19, No. 10 (June 26).

Einsichten. Aus den Schriften gesammelt. Wiesbaden: Insel Verlag.

For the Sake of Heaven. Translated by Ludwig Lewisohn. Second edition with new foreword. New York: Harper & Brothers.

"Forewoard" to Erick Gutkind, *Community and Environment.* London: Watts.

"Geleitwort," in Ludwig Strauss, *Wintersaat; ein Buch aus Sätzen.* Zürich: Manesse.

"Geltung und Grenze des politischen Prinzips" in *Gedenkschrift zur Verleihung des Hansischen Goethe-Preises 1951 der gemeinnützigen Stiftung F.V.S. zu Hamburg an* M. B., *überreicht am 24. Juni 1953.* (Hamburg), pp. 9-20. (Also in *Frankfurter Hefte* Vol. 8, No. 9 [September] and *Neue Schweizer Rundschau* N. F. XXI, 5 [September].)

Good and Evil. Two Interpretations. New York: Charles Schribner's Sons. Includes *Right and Wrong* and *Images of Good and Evil.*

Gottesfinsternis. Zürich: Manesse Verlag. (For contents see *Eclipse of God* [1952].)

"Hasheilah hanisteret" (in Hebrew), *Orot,* No. 2, Elul (from "Bemashber haruach").

"Hassischah haamitit veefscharut leschalom" (in Hebrew), *Davar* (Friedenspreis).

Hinweise, Gesammelte Essays (1909-1953). Zürich: Manesse Verlag. Includes "Vorwort," "Bücher un Menschen" (1947), "Leistung und Dasein" (1914), "Der Dämon im Traum" (1914), "Der Altar" (1914), "Bruder Leib" (1914), "Mit einem Monisten" (1914), "Die Lehre vom Tao" (1909), "Das Epos des Zauberers" (1913), "Die Vorurteile der Jugend" (1937), "An das Gleichzeitige" (1914), "Die Forderung des Geistes und die geschichtliche Wirklichkeit" (1938), "Geschehende Geschichte" (1933), "Biblisches Führertum" (1928), "Falsche Propheten" (1941), "Was soll mit den Zehn Geboten geschehen?" (1929), "Mein Weg zum

Chassidismus" (1918), "Drama und Theater" (1925), "Das Raumproblem der Bühne" (1913), "Das Reinmenschliche" (1949), "Zu Bergsons Begriff der Intuition" (1943), "Alfred Mombert" (1922), "Moritz Heimann" (1912), "Franz Rosenzweig" (1930), "Erinnerung an einen Tod" (1929), "Drei Sätze eines religiösen Sozialismus" (1928), "Nationalismus" (1921), "Gandhi, die Politik und wir" (1930), "Was ist zu tun?" (1919), "Volk und Führer" (1942), "Hoffnung für diese Stunde" (1952), "Abstrakt und Kongret" (1952), "Geltung und Grenze des politischen Prinzips" (1947).

"Rede über das Erzieherische," in Wilhelm, Flitner. *Die Erziehung; Pädagogen und Philosophen über die Erziehung und ihre Probleme.* Wiesbaden: Dieterich.

Reden über Erziehung. Heidelberg: Verlag Lambert Schneider. Includes "Vorwort," "Über das Erzieherische," "Buildung und Weltanschauung," and "Über Charaktererziehung."

"Sur la mer est ton Chemin" in *Evidences,* Vol. 5, No. 36 (December) (from *Bein Am learzo*).

"Über ein Zusammentreffen und was darauf folgte," *Mitteilungsblatt,* Vol. 21, No. 13/14 (March 30).

"Zwischen Religion und Philosophie" (answer to Hugo Bergmann's criticism of *Eclipse of God*), *Neue Wege,* Vol. 47, No. 11/12 (November/December), pp. 436-439.

1954

"Aus dem Werk: Uber den Zionismus. Wiedergeburt des Dialogs. Eine Bekehrung. Versöhnung. Gott," in Hans Schwerte; Wilhelm Spengler *Denker und Deuter im heutigen Europa: England, Frankreich, Spanien und Portugal, Italien, Osteuropa.* (Martin Buber by Hans Joachim Schoeps). Oldenburg: G. Stalling. Gestalten unserer Zeit, 2.

"Christus, Chassidismus, Gnosis. Einige Bemerkungen" (Reply to an article by Rudolph Pannwitz in *Merkur,* September

1954, *Merkur* (Munich), Vol. 8, No. 80 (October). (Included in translation in *The Origin and Meaning of Hasidism* [1960].)

"Dat umussar" (in Hebrew), *Iyyun*, No. 5.

"Elemente des Zwischenmenschlichen," *Merkur*, February, *Neue Schweizer Rundschau* (Zurich), Neue Folge, Vol. 21, No. 10 (February), pp. 593-608. Also included in *Die Schriften über das dialogische Prinzip* (1954).

"Ewige Feindschaft? Hans Klee and M. B. über das Verhältnis zwischen Juden und Deutschen," *Freiburger Rundbrief*, Vol. 7, No. 25/28 (September).

(in cooperation with Franz Rosenzweig.) *Die fünf Bücher der Weisung. (Die Schrift)* revised edition. Köln und Olten: Jakob Hegner Verlag.

Godsverduistering; beschouwingen over de betrekking tussen religie en filosofie. Translated by K. H. Kroon. Utrecht: E. J. Bijleveld. *(Eclipse of God).*

"Humanist ivrit—al mahutah shel hatarbut" (in Hebrew), *Machshavot vedeiot*, collected and edited by I. Becker and Sh. Shapan. Tel Aviv: Yaveneh.

"Letters to Franz Rosenzweig on the Law," in Franz Rosenzweig, *On Jewish Education.* Edited by Nahum N. Glatzer. New York: The Noonday Press.

"Mellan Religion Och Filosofi," *Judisk tidskrift*, Vol. 27, No. 1 (January).

(Message), *Pulpit digest*, Vol. 34, No. 194 (June) (Special issue on the hydrogen cobalt bomb). Translated by Maurice Friedman.

"Prophetie, Apokalyptik und die geschichtliche Stunde," *Merkur,* Vol. 8, No. 12 (December). *Neue Schweizer Rundschau* N.F. XXII, 8.

"Samuel und die Lade," in *Essays Presented to Leo Baeck on His Eightieth Birthday.* London: East and West Library. (A chapter from *Der Gesalbte*, the unfinished sequel to *Königtum Gottes*, 1936.)

Die Schriften über das dialogische Prinzip. Heidelberg: Verlag Lambert Schneider. Includes *Ich und Du, Zwiesprache, Die Frage an den Einzelnen,* "Elemente des Zwischennmenschlichen," and "Nachwort," the last two not previously published in book form, the last an important historical survey published here for the first time.

"Die Wahre Geschichte, zu Kurt Blumenfelds 70. Geburtstag," *Mitteilungsblatt,* Vol. 22, No. 22 (May 28).

Zu einer neuen Verdeutschung der Schrift. Beilage zu dem Werk "Die Fünf Bücher der Weisung" verdeutscht von Martin Buber in Gemeinschaft mit Franz Rosenzweig. Köln and Olten: Jakob Hegner Verlag.

"Zur Klärung," *Mitteilungsblatt,* Vol. 22, No. 23 (June 4).

1955

"Bein adam lehavero" (in Hebrew), *Achsania,* No. 1, Sivan.

Between Man and Man. Translated by Ronald Gregor Smith. Boston: Beacon Paperback.

(in cooperation with Franz Rosenzweig) *Bücher der Geschichte.* Köln and Olten: Jakob Hegner Verlag.

Caminos de Utopia, Translated by J. Rovira Armengol. Mexico: Fondo de Cultura económica. Breviarios del Fondo de Cultura económica, 104.

Eclipse de Dios; estudios sobre las relaciones entre religion y filosofía, Translated by Luis Fabricant. Buenos Aires: Galatea-Nueva Visión, = Ideas de nuestro tempo.

En la encrucijada; tres conferencias sobre el judaismo. (Versión castellana de Luis Fabricant.) Buenos Aires: Sociedad hebraica argentina (*At the Turning*).

"Epos hakosem" (in Hebrew), "Bechinot," No. 8, Nisan. (Introduction to *Kalevala*).Translated by Shaul Tchernikowsky.

Die Geschicten des Rabbi Nachman. Revised edition. Frankfurt am Main and Hamburg: Fischer Bücherei.

"God and the soul," in Dagobert D. Runes, *Treasury of Philosophy.* New York: The Philosophical Library.

"Hoffnung für diese Stunde," *Universitas*, Vol. 10, No. 1 (January).

The Legend of the Baal-Shem. Translated by Maurice S. Friedman. New York: Harper & Brothers. London: East and West Library, 1956.

Die Legende des Baalschem. Revised new edition. Manesse Bibliothek der Weltliteratur. Zürich: Manesse Verlag.

Der Mensch und sein Gebild. Heidelberg: Verlag Lambert Schneider.

"Ein Realist des Geistes," *Ehrfurcht vor dem Leben: Albert Schweitzer. Eine Freundesgabe zu seinem 80. Geburtstag*. Bern: P. Haupt.

"A Realist of the Spirit." Translated by Maurice Friedman, in *To Dr. Albert Schweitzer; a Festschrift commemorating his 80th birthday from a few of his friends*. January 14, 1955. Evanston (Ill.), Friends of Albert Schweitzer. (ed. Homer Jack).

Sehertum. Anfang und Ausgang ("Abraham der Seher" and "Prophetie, Apokalyptik und die Geschichtliche Stunde"). Köln: Jakob Hegner.

"Über das Erzieherische," *Pädagogische Blätter*, Vol. 6, No. 13/14 (July).

"Versuch einer Auskunft" in *Wegweiser in der Zeitwende*. Edited by Elga Kern. Munich, Basle: Ernst Reinhardt Verlag, pp. 264 ff.

"We need the Arabs, they need us! Interview with M. B.," *Frontpage*, Vol. 2, No. 3 (Jan. 20).

1956

"Abraham the Seer." Translated by Sophie Meyer. *Judaism*, Vol. 5, No. 4 (Fall).

"Eine Auswahl," *Wort in der Zeit,* Vol. 2, No. 11 (November).

"Character change and social experiment, in Israel," edited by

Maurice Friedman, in Moshe Davis, *Israel, its Role in Civilization*. New York: Seminary Israel Institute.

"Der Chassidismus und der abendländische Mensch," *Merkur*, Vol. 10, No. 10 (October).

"Die Erzählung von Sauls Königswahl," *Vetus Testamentum*, Vol. 6, No. 2 (April).

"Für das Ganze Zeugend," AJR *Information*, Vol. 11, No. 12 (December) (supplement in memory of Leo Baeck . . .).

"Dem Gemeinschaftlichen folgen." *Die Neue Rundschau*, Vol. 67, No. 4 (December).

"Greetings to Dr. Mordecai M. Kaplan," *The Reconstructionist*, Vol. 22, No. 6 (May 4).

"Haadam haboreach" (in Hebrew), *Molad*, No. 14 (December). ("Dem Gemeinschaftlichen folgen.")

"Jugend und Religion.—Harmonie mit dem Nächsten. Ein kleiner Auszug." *Einkland* 3 (July).

"Réalité légendaire; le Tsaddik dans sa communauté." (Traduit par Yohanan Lavi), in *Renaissance*, Vol. 2, No. 7 (November).

Königtum Gottes. Third revised edition. Heidelberg: Verlag Lambert Schneider.

"Rosenzweig und die Existenz," *Mitteilungsblatt*, Vol. 24, No. 52 (Dec. 28).

The Tales of Rabbi Nachman. Translated by Maurice Friedman. New York: The Horizon Press.

The Writings of Martin Buber. Selected, edited, and introduced by Will Herberg. New York: Meridian Books.

1957

"Distance and Relation." Translated by Ronald Gregor Smith. *Psychiatry*, Vol. 20, No. 2 (May), pp. 97-104. (Later included in *The Knowledge of Man* [1966].)

Eclipse of God. Studies in the Relation between Religion and

Philosophy. Translated by Maurice Friedman, et al. New York: Harper Torchbooks (paperback).

"Elements of the Interhuman." Translated by Ronald Gregor Smith, *Psychiatry*, Vol. 20, No. 2 (May), pp. 105-129. (Later included in *The Knowledge of Man* [1966].)

"Erinnerung," *Die Neue Rundschau*, Vol. 68, No. 4, pp. 575 ff.

"Die Erwählung Israels," *Quatember*, Evangelische Jahresbriefe 6, XXI, No. 3, 1956-1957 (June), pp. 136-145.

Fourth William Allen White Memorial Lectures (Introduction by Leslie H. Farber, "Distance and Relation," "Elements of the Interhuman," "Guilt and Guilt-Feelings"). Reprints from *Psychiatry*, 1610 New Hampshire Avenue, N.W., Washington, D.C. 20009

Gog und Magog; eine Chronik. Frankfurt a. M.: Fischer, Fischer Bücherei, 174.

"Guilt and Guilt-Feelings." Translated by Maurice Friedman. *Psychiatry*, Vol. 20, No. 2 (May), pp. 114-129. Also in *Cross Currents*, 1958. (Later included in *The Knowledge of Man* [1966].)

"Haltet ein!". *Neue Wege*, Vol. 51, No. 6 (August).

"Le Hassidisme et l'homme d'Occident." in *Mélanges de philosophie et de littérature juives* 1/2; 1956-1957 (Institut international d'études hébraïques). Paris: Presses Universitaires de France.

"Hermann Hesses Dienst am Geist," *Neue Deutsche Hefte* No. 37 (August), pp. 387-393.

Moïse. Traduit de l'allemand par Albert Kohn. Paris: Presses Universitaires de France, Sinaï, collection des sources d'Israël.

Pointing the Way: Collected Essays. Translated and edited by Maurice Friedman. New York: Harper & Brothers; London: Routledge & Kegan Paul. Includes most of the essays in *Hinweise* (1953) plus "Healing through Meeting," "China and Us," "Education and World-View," "A Letter to

Gandhi," "Society and the State," "Prophecy, Apocalyptic, and the Historical Hour," and "Genuine Dialogue and the Possibilities of Peace." Does not include from *Hinweise* "Das Epos des Zauberers," "Mein Weg zum Chassidismus," "Alfred Mombert," "Moritz Heinmann," or the essays published in *Israel and the World*.

"Prophetie et Apocalypse." Traduit par Marthe Robert. *Evidences*, Vol. 9, No. 68 (December).

"Schuld und Schuldgefühle. (Vorlesung, gehalten an der School for Psychiatry in Washington im April 1957)," *Merkur*, Vol. 11, No. 8 (August).

De Vraag naar de mens; het anthropologisch probleem historisch en dialogisch ontvouwd. Translated by I. J. Van Houte. Utrecht: E. J. Bijleveld.

1958

"Aus der Übersetzung der Bibel" (Neviim, Tehillim) in Rudolf Jockel, *Die Lebenden Religionen*. Berlin and Darmstadt: Deutsche Buch-Gemeinschaft, C. A. Koch's Verlag Nachf.

"Born of Envy," *Chelsea Review*, Summer.

Das Buch der Preisungen. Köln and Olten: Jakob Hegner.

Bücher der Kündung. Köln and Olten: Jakob Hegner.

"Bücher und Menschen," Neue Wege, February.

"Es Menester Seguir lo Comun al Hombre," in *Entregas de La Licorne*. Ed. Susanna Soca, printed in Uraguary, 2a Epoca—Vol. 5, No. 11.

For the Sake of Heaven. 2nd Ed. with New Foreword. Translated by Ludwig Lewisohn. New York: Meridian Books-Jewish Publication Society (paperback).

Gog et Magog. Translated by Hans Loewenson-Lavi. Paris: Gallimard.

Hasidism and Modern Man. Edited and translated by Maurice Friedman. With an Editor's Introduction. New York: The Horizon Press. Includes "Hasidism and Modern Man"

(1957), "My Way to Hasidism" (1918), "The Life of the Hasidim" (from *The Legend of the Baal-Shem* [1955]), *The Way of Man, According to the Teachings of Hasidism* (1950), *The Baal-Shem-Tov's Instruction in Intercourse with God* (1928), and "Love of God and Love of Neighbor" (1943).)

"Hasidism and Modern Man" in *Between East and West*. London: East and West Library.

"Hataamula vehacinuch" (in Hebrew), *Hed hachinuch* (Dec. 31).

I and Thou. Second Edition with important Postscript by the Author. Translated by Ronald Gregor Smith. New York: Charles Schribner's Sons.

Ich und Du. Nachworterweiterte. Heidelberg: Verlag Lambert Schneider.

"Il Comando dello spirito e la via attuale d'Israele" in *Israel*. Il Ponte, December.

"Israel and the Command of the Spirit." Translated by Maurice Friedman, *Congress Weekly*, Vol. 25, No. 14 (Sept. 8), pp. 10 ff.

"It is now high time" in *London Letter*.

"Kleiner Beitrag" in *Agora. Eine Schriftenreihe*, ed. Manfred Schlösser and Hans-Rolf Ropertz. In association with the Ludwig-Georgs-Gymnasium, Darmstadt and the Verein der Freunde des Ludwig-Georgs Gymnasiums, Vol. 4, No. 11 (November) Darmstadt: Wissenschaftliche Buch Gesellschaft.

Moses. New York: Harper Torchbooks (paperback).

Paths in Utopia. Translated by R. D. C. Hull. With Introduction by Ephraim Fischoff. Boston: Beacon Paperbacks.

Schuld und Schuldgefühle. Heidelberg: Verlag Lambert Schneider.

"Sur les Récits Hassidiques" in *La Table Ronde* (March).

Tales of Angels, Spirits & Demons. Translated by David Antin and Jerome Rothenberg. New York: Hawk's Well Press.

To Hallow This Life, An Anthology. Edited with Introduction by Jacob Trapp. New York: Harper & Brothers.

"Der Weg Israels (zur Klärung)" in *Mitteilungsblatt* (Oct. 3).

"What is common to all." Translated by Maurice Friedman. *Review of Metaphysics*, Vol. 11, No. 3 (March), pp. 359-379. (Later included in *The Knowledge of Man* [1966].)

1959

"Aus erster Hand, ein Gespräch mit Thilo Koch," Nord und Westdeutscher Rundfunkverband-Fernsehen-Hamburg-Lokstedt, (May 25).

"Ein Beispiel. Zu den Landschaften Leopold Krakauers," *Merkur*, 139, Vol. 13, No. 9 (September), pp. 840 ff.

Besod Ssiach (in Hebrew), Jerusalem: Mosad Bialik. (Dialogical writings.)

(editor) Entsiklopedyah Hainochit (in Hebrew) (educational encyclopedia of Jewish and general education. Martin Buber, editor-in-chief.) Jerusalem: Misrad Hahinuk vHatarbut.

"Hebrew Humanism" in Adrienne Koch, *Philosophy for a Time of Crisis*. New York: E. P. Dutton & Co.

"Hoffnung für diese Stunde" in *Reden, die die Welt bewegten*. Ed. Karl Heinrich Peter. Stuttgart: Cotta-Verlag.

I and Thou. 2nd ed. with Postscript by Author added. Translated by Ronald Gregor Smith. Edinburgh: T. & T. Clark.

"I and Thou" in Yervant H. Krikorian and Abraham Edel, editors, *Contemporary Philosophic Problems. Selected Readings*. New York: The Macmillan Co.

Ik en Gij. Translated by I. J. Van Houte. Utrecht: Erven J. Bijleveld.

Il Principio Dialogico. Translated by Paoli Facchi and Ursula Schnabel. Roma: Edizioni di Communita. (*Die Schriften über das dialogische Prinzip* without the "Nachwort.")

"Israel's Mission and Zion." *Forum, for the Problems of Zionism, Jewry, and the State of Israel*, Vol. 4 (Spring), "Proceedings of the Jerusalem Ideological Conference." Ed.

"Shtei Pegishot" (in Hebrew), *Molad*, No. 163 (June-July) ("Zwei Begegnungen").

"Schuld und Schuldgefühle" in *Der leidende Mensch*, Vol. I—*Wege der Forschung*. Darmstadt: Wissenschaftliche Buchgesellschaft.

"Seit ein Gespräch wir sind, Ludwig Strauss zum Gedächtnis" in *Holderlin-Jahrbuch*, 1958-1960. Vol. 11; Tübingen: J.C.B. Mohr (Paul Siebeck).

"Symbolic and Sacramental Existence in Judaism." Translated by Ralph Manheim. In *Spiritual Disciplines*, Volume IV of *Papers from the Eranos Yearbooks*. Bollingen Series XXX. New York: Pantheon Books, pp. 168-185.

Urdistanz und Beziehung. Second edition. Heidelberg: Lambert Schneider.

"La Via della Communita" in *Tempo Presente* (Gennaio). ("Dem Gemeinschaftliche folgen.")

Der Weg des Menschen nach der chassidischen Lehre. Third edition. Heidelberg: Lambert Schneider.

"Das Wort, das gesprochen wird," in *Wort und Wirklichkeit*, Vol. VI of *Gestalt und Gedanke*, Jahrbuch der Bayerischen Akademie der schönen Künste. Munich: R. Oldenburg Verlag.

"Zwei Begegnungen," *Merkur*, No. 148 (June). (Two chapters from the "Autobiographical Fragments" of this volume.)

1961

Am ve'olam (in Hebrew) ("A People and the World"). Jerusalem: Sifriah Zionit (second volume of essays of Judaism).

Between Man and Man. Translated by Ronald Gregor Smith. London: Collins. The Fontana Library, (paperback).

"Books and People." Translated by Harry Zohn, *The Jewish Advocate* (Boston).

"Brief an Gandhi" in *Juden, Palästina, Araber*. Munich: Ner-Tamid-Verlag.

"Der Chassidismus und die Krise des abendländischen Menschen," in *Juden, Christen, Deutsche*. Edited by Hans-Jürgen Schultz. Stuttgart: Kreuz-Verlag.

"Dankesrede zum Münchener Kulturpreis" in *München ehrt Martin Buber*. Munich: Ner-Tamid-Verlag.

Eclissi di Dio. Edizioni Communita, Milan. (*Gottesfinsternis*)

"Erinnerung" in *Im Zeichen der Hoffnung*, ed. by Erwin de Haar. Munich: Max Huber Verlag.

Good and Evil. Two Interpretations. New York: Scribner's Paperbacks.

"Die Juden in der USSR," in *Die Sowjets und das Judentum*, (Vom Gestern zum Morgan, Zeitgeschichtliche Schriftenreihe), ed. Hans Lamm. Munich and Frankfurt: Ner-Tamid-Verlag.

"Robert Weltsch zum 70. Geburtstag," *Mitteilungsblatt*, June 16.

"Schlussbemerkungen," in *'Die Schrift'—Zum Abschluss ihrer Verdeut-schung*. Sonderdruck überreicht vom "Mitteilungsblatt" (MB) des Irgun Olej Merkas Europa. Tel Aviv: Biaton Publishing Co., pp. 8 ff.

Tales of the Hasidim, The Early Masters. Translated by Olga Marx. New York: Schocken Books (paperback).

Tales of the Hasidim, The Later Masters. Translated by Olga Marx. New York: Schocken Books (paperback edition).

Two Types of Faith. Translated by Norman P. Goldhawk. New York: Harper Torchbooks (paperback).

"Wie kann Gemeinschaft werden?" (1930), reprinted in *Munchen ehrt Martin Buber*. Munich: Ner-Tamid-Verlag.

"The word that is spoken." Translated by Maurice Friedman. *Modern Age* (Chicago), Fall, Vol. 5, No. 4. (Later included in *The Knowledge of Man* [1966].)

1962

Logos. Zwei Reden. Heidelberg: Verlag Lambert Schneider.

Nathan Rotenstreich, Sulamith Schwartz Nardi, Zalman Shazar. Jerusalem: Publishing Department of the Jewish Agency, pp. 145 ff.

Pfade in Utopia. Japanese translation by Susuma Hasegawa. Tokyo: Riso-sha Co.

Steeg'n in Utopia (Yiddish Edition). Buenos Aires: Buchgemeinschaft bei de "jiddischer razionalistascher Gesellschaft."

Teudah v-jeud (in Hebrew), Jerusalem: Sifriah Zionit. First volume of essays on Judaism.

La Vie en Dialogue. Translated by Hans Loewenson-Lavi. Paris: Aubier, Éditions Montaigne.

The Way of Man, according to the Teachings of Hasidism. Foreword by Maurice Friedman. Wallingford, Pennsylvania: Pendle Hill Pamphlet No. 106.

1960

Begegnung. Autobiographische Fragmente. Ed. by Paul Arthur Schilpp and Maurice Friedman. Stuttgart: W. Kohlhammer Verlag. (The "Autobiographical Fragments" from *The Philosophy of Martin Buber* volume of *The Library of Living Philosophers*.)

Brief (Letter) in *Erziehung zur Humanität. Paul Geheeb zum 90. Geburstag.*

"Discourse sur la situation des Juifs en Union Soviétique," *La Terre Retrouvée*, (September), et l'*Arche*, (October).

"Geheimnis einer Einheit, Herman Stehr," *Jahresgabe*, Stuttgart: Brentanoverlag. (Reprint from "Hermann Stehr, sein Werk und seine Welt" [1924]).

"Gruss und Willkommen (Begrüssung Theodore Heuss von der Hebraischen Universität)" in *Staat und Volk im Werden*, ed. by Theodor Heuss. Munich: Ner-Tamid Verlag.

"Hoffnung für diese Stunde" in *Wo stehen wir heute?* ed. by H. Walter Bähr. Gütersloh: Bertelsmann Verlag.

I and Thou. 2nd Edition with Postscript Added. Translated by Ronald Gregor Smith. New York: Scribner's Paperback.

"Ich und Du" in *Sinn und Sein*, ed. Richard Wisser. Tübingen: Max Niemeyer Verlag. (The Postscript of the 1958 edition).

"Neum al Yehudei Brit-Hamoezot" (in Hebrew), *Chasut*, Hoveret h' (5), Kislev 5721, Sifria Zionite, Bearichat Prof. Rotenstreich and Z. Shazar.

"Neum al Yehudei Brit-Hamoezot" (in Hebrew), *Gesher*, Revuon Lesheilot Hajehaumah (Quarterly Review of the Nation's Problems). Published by the Israel Executive of the World Jewish Congress Editorial Board. 1 Ben Yehuda, Jerusalem Sixth Year (25) 4.

The Origin and Meaning of Hasidism. Ed. and trans. with an Editor's Introduction by Maurice Friedman. New York: The Horizon Press. Includes "The Beginnings" (1943), "The Foundation Stone" (1943), "Spinoza, Sabbatai Zvi, and the Baal-Shem" (1927), "Symbolic and Sacramental Existence" Movement" (1921), "Symbolic and Sacramental Existence" [1934] "God and the Soul" (1943), "Redemption" (1947), "The Place of Hasidism in the History of Religion" (1943), "Christ, Hasidism, Gnosis" (1954).

"Productivity and Existence." (From *Pointing the Way*, translated by Maurice Friedman), in Maurice A. Stein, Arthur J. Vidick, David M. White, editors, *Identity and Anxiety; Survival of the Person in a Mass Society*. Glencoe, Illinois: The Free Press, pp. 628-632.

The Prophetic Faith. Translated by Carlyle Witton-Davies. New York: Harper's Torchbooks (paperback).

Que es el Hombre, 4th ed. Mexico and Buenos Aires: Fondo de Cultura Económica.

Includes "Das Wort, das gesprochen wird" and "Dem Gemeinschaftlichen folgen."

Die Schrift. Translation of the Bible from Hebrew into German by Martin Buber in cooperation with Franz Rosenzweig. Revised edition. 4 vols.: *Die fünf Bücher der Weisung* (1954), *Bücher der Kundung* (1958), *Die Schriftwerke* (1961). Köln and Olten: Jakob Hegner Verlag.

Die Schriftwerke. Revised edition. Köln and Olten: Jakob Hegner.

The Tales of Rabbi Nachman. Translated by Maurice Friedman. Bloomington, Indiana: Indiana University Press, Midland Books (paperback).

Werke. Erster Band—*Schriften zur Philosophie*. Munich and Heidelberg: Kösel Verlag and Lambert Schneider. Includes *Daniel, Ich und Du, Zwiesprache, Die Frage an den Einzelnen, Elemente des Zwischenmenschlichen, Zur Geschichte des dialogischen Prinzips, Urdistanz und Beziehung, Der Mensch und sein Gebild, Das Wort, das gesprochen wird, Dem Gemeinschaftlichen folgen, Schuld und Schuldgefühle, Gottesfinsternis, Betrachtungen zur Beziehung zwischen Religion und Philosophie, Bilder von Gut und Bose, Zwei Glaubensweisen, Reden über Erziehung, Pfade in Utopia, Zwischen Gesellschaft und Staat,* "Die Lehre von Tao," "Die Forderung des Geistes und die geschichtliche Wirklichkeit," "Zu Bergsons Begriff der Intuition," "Gandhi, die Politik und wir," "Geltung und Grenze des politischen Prinzips," "Aus einer philophischen Reschenschaft" (the first section of Buber's responses to critics in the Buber volume of *The Library of Living Philosophers*).

Zur Verdeutschung des letzten Bandes der Schrift. Beilage zu "Die Schriftwerke." Köln & Olten: Jakob Hegner.

1963

"Autobiographische Fragmente" and "Responsa" in *Die*

Philosophie Martin Bubers (Philosophen des XX. *Jahrhunderts).* Eds. Paul Arthur Schilpp and Maurice Friedman. Stuttgart: W. Kohlhammer Verlag.

Elija. Ein Mysterienspiel. Heidelberg: Verlag Lambert Schneider.

Israel and the World. Essays in a Time of Crisis. New York: Schocken Paperbacks. (The 1948 original plus "Israel and the Command of the Spirit" [1958] translated by Maurice Friedman, and "Israel's Mission and Zion" [1957].)

Der Jude und sein Judentum. Gesammelte Aufsätze und Reden. Mit einer Einleitung von Robert Weltsch. Köln: Joseph Melzer Verlag. Includes I. Reden über das Judentum: Die frühen Reden and An der Wende; II. Die Grundlagen: Der Glaube des Judentums, Die Brennpunkte der jüdischen Seele, Freiheit und Aufgabe, Der Jude in der Welt, Pharisäertum, Bericht und Berichtigung, Das Judentum und die neue Weltfrage, Das Gestaltende, Im Anfang; III. Wiedergeburt: Regeneration eines Volkstums, Renaissance und Bewegung, Völker, Staaten und Zion, Nationalismus, Zur Geschichte der nationalen Ideen, Jüdisches Nationalheim und nationale Politik in Palästina, Wann denn?, Frage und Antwort, Zweierlei Zionismus, Der Chaluz und seine Welt, Arbeitsglaube, Wie kann Gemeinschaft werden?, Warum muss der Aufbau Palästinas ein sozialistischer sein?, Zion und die Gola; IV. Zur Geschichte des Zionismus: Der Anfang der nationalen Idee, Der Erste der Letzten, Die drängende Stunde, Die Lehre vom Zentrum, Die Erneuerung der Heiligkeit, Ein Träger der Verwirklichung; V. Situationen: Rede auf dem 12. Zionistenkongress, Kongressnotizen zur zionistischen Politik, Selbstbesinnung, Ein politischer Faktor, Die Eroberung Palästinas, Vor der Entscheidung, In später Stunde, Rede auf dem 16. Zionistenkongress, Gegen die Untreue, Pseudo-Simsonismus, Über ein Zusammentreffen und was darauf folgte, Der Weg Israels, Die Sowjets und das Judentum; VI. In der Krisis: Der jüdische Mensch von heute, Kirche, Staat, Volk, Judentum, Die Mächtigkeit des Geistes, Das Erste, Die Kinder, Gericht und Erneuerung, Das Haltende, Worauf es ankommt, Ein Spruch des Maimuni, Erkenntnis tut not, Unser Bildungsziel, Aufgaben jüdischer Volkserziehung, Jüdische Erwachsenenbildung, Entwürfe und Programme, Brief en Ernst Michel, Offener Brief an Gerhard Kittel, Zu Gehard Kittels Antwort, Brief an Gandhi, Das Ende der deutsch-jüdischen Symbiose, Sie und wir, Schweigen und Schreien; VII. Erziehung und Kulturarbeit: An die Prager Freunde, Die Lehre und die Tat, Kulturarbeit, Volkserziegung als unsere Aufgabe, Universität und Volkshochschule, Jüdisch Leben, Zion und die Jugend, Die Vorurteile der Jugend, Die hebräische Sprache, Hebräischer Humanismus, Warum gelernt werden soll, Grau nach der Welt, Ha-bima!, Drei Stationen; VIII. Gestalten: Vertrauen, Der Wägende, Achad-Haam-Gedenkrede in Berlin, Achad-Haam-Gedenkrede in Basel, Zwei hebräische Bücher, Der wahre Lehrer, Der Acker und die Sterne, Theodor Herzl, Herzl und die Historie, Er und wir, Sache und Person, Herzl vor der Palästina-Karte, Der Dichter und die Nation, Die Tränen, Philon und Cohen, Für die Sache der Treue, Franz Rosenzweig, Rosenzweig und die Existenz.

Martin Buber. Herausgegeben von Paul Arthur Schilpp und Maurice Friedman. Stuttgart: W. Kohlhammer Verlag. xiv + 660 pp. (The German edition of *The Philosophy of Martin Buber*, Vol. 12 in *The Library of Living Philosophers*.) English edition in 1966.

Pointing the Way. Collected Essays. Edited and translated with an Editor's Introduction by Maurice Friedman. New York: Harper Torchbooks (paperback).

Werke. Dritter Band—*Schriften zum Chassidismus.* Munich and Heidelberg: Kösel Verlag and Verlag Lambert Schneider. Includes *Die Erzählungen der Chassidim, Die chassidische Botschaft, Der Weg des Menschen nach der chassidischen Lehre, Mein Weg zum Chassidismus*, "Der Chassidismus und der abendländische Mensch," "Christus, Chassidismus, Gnosis," *Des Baal-Schem-Tow Unterweisung im Umgang mit Gott*, "Einleitung zu Nachman," "Ein Zaddik kommt ins Land," "Einleitung zu Baal-Schem," *Gog und Magog.*

1964

"Church, State, Nation, Jewry." Translated by William Hallo with an Introductory Note by Maurice Friedman in *Christianity: Some Non-Christian Appraisals*, edited by David W. McKain with an Introduction by Robert Lawson Slater. New York: McGraw-Hill Paperbacks, pp. 174-188.

Daniel, Dialogues on Realization. Edited and translated with an Introductory Essay by Maurice Friedman. New York: Holt, Rinehart & Winston, Inc.

"Responsa" in "Martin Buber" Section, conducted, edited, and translated by Maurice Friedman, of *Philosophical Interrogations.* Ed. Sidney and Beatrice Rome. New York: Holt, Rinehart & Winston, Inc.

Selections from eighteen of Buber's works in *The Worlds of Existentialism: A Critical Reader.* Edited with Introductions and A Conclusion by Maurice Friedman. New York: Random House. Part I—Forerunners, pp. 42-48; Part II—Phenomenology and Ontology, pp. 105-107; Part III—The Existential Subject, p. 160-167; Part IV—Intersubjectivity, pp. 216-235; Part V—Atheist, Humanist, and Religious Existentialism, pp. 306-318; Part VI—Existentialism and Psychotheraphy, pp. 385-396, 485-497; Part VII—Issues and Conclusions, p. 535.

The Way of Man, according to the Teachings of Hasidism. London: Collins Books. Also reprinted in Walter Kaufmann, *Religion from Tolstoy to Camus.* New York: Harper Torchbooks (paperback).

Weke. Zweiter Band—*Schriften zur Bibel.* Munich and Heidelberg: Kösel-Verlag and Verlag Lambert Schneider.

Includes *Moses, Der Glaube der Propheten, Königtum Gottes, Der Gesalbte* (unpublished up till now), "Der Mensch von heute und die jüdische Bibel," "Abraham der Seher," "Was soll mit den zehn Geboten geschehen?," "Biblisches Führertum," "Weisheit und Tat der Frauen," "Prophetie und Apokalyptik," "Falsche Propheten," *Recht und Unrecht. Deutung einiger Psalmen, Biblisches Zeugnis* (from *Israel und Palästina*), "Geschehende Geschichte," "Die Erwählung Israels," "Nachahmung Gottes," "Die Götter der Völker und Gott," "Biblischer Humanismus," *Die Schrift und ihre Verdeutschung*: "Die Sprache der Botschaft," "Über die Wortwahl in einer Verdeutschung der Schrift," "Leitwortstil in der Erzählung des Pentateuchs," "Das Leitwort und der Formtypus der Rede," "Zur Verdeutschung der Preisungen," "Zur Verdeutschung der Gleichsprüche," "Zur Verdeutschung des Buches Ijob (Hiob)," "Zum Abschluss," "Ein Hinweis für Bibelkurse"; *Elija. Ein Mysterienspiel.*

Between Man and Man. New edition with an Introduction by Maurice Friedman. With an Afterword by the Author on "The History of the Dialogical Principle, translated by Maurice Friedman. Translated (except for the Afterword) by Ronald Gregor Smith. New York: Macmillan Paperbacks.

Daniel. Dialogues on Realization. Edited and translated with an Introductory Essay by Maurice Friedman. New York: McGraw-Hill Paperbacks.

Elijah. A Mystery Play. Selections from Scenes 1, 3, 4, 6, 8, 10, 11, 16, 18, 20, 22, 23. Translated by Maurice Friedman, *Judaism*, Vol. 14, No. 3 (Summer), pp. 260-266.

The Knowledge of Man. Edited with an Introductory Essay by Maurice Friedman, Translated by Maurice Friedman and Ronald Gregor Smith. London: George Allen & Unwin. (Includes "Distance and Relation," "Elements of the Interhuman," "What Is Common to All," "The Word That

Is Spoken," "Guilt and Guilt Feelings," "Man and His Image-Work," and "Dialogue between Martin Buber and Carl R. Rogers."

Nachlese. Heidelberg: Verlag Lambert Schneider. Includes many poems, short tributes, fragments, and essays selected by Buber himself before his death. Previously published in German: "Bekenntnis des Schriftstellers" (1945), "Erinnerung" (1957), "Aus einem Schreiben an das 'Internationale Institut für Philosophie' (Amsterdam)" (1917), "Elijahu" (1903), "Das Wort an Elijahu" (1904), "Aus dem Zyklus 'Geist der Herr' ": "Der Jünger" and "Die Magier" (1901), "Gewalt und Liebe" (1926), "Das dämonische Buch" (1924), "Am Tag der Rückschau" (1928), "Geister und Menschen" (1961), "Ein Realist des Geistes" (1955), Über Richard Beer-Hofmann" (1962), "Hermann Hesses Dienst am Geist" (1957), "Authentische Zwiesprachigkeit" (1963), "Seit ein Gespräch wir sind" (1957), "Bemerkungen zur Gemeinschaftsidee" (1931), "Der dritte Tischfuss" (1925), "Erziehen" (1960), "Die Aufgabe" (1922), "Über den Kontakt" (1950), "Stil und Unterricht" (1921), "Ein Beispiel" (1959), "Religion und Gottesherrschaft" (1923), "Fragmente über Offenbarung" (1964), "Gläubiger Humanismus" (1963), "Haus Gottess" (1932), "Religiöse Erziehung" (1930), "Über Religionswissenschaft" (1928), "Philosophische und religiöse Weltanschauung" (1928), "Zur Situation der Philosophie" (1948), "Heilung aus der Begegnung" (1951), "Politik aus dem Glauben" (1933), "Zu Zwei Burckhardt-Worten" (1961), "Ein Gespräch mit Tagore" (1950), "China und Wir" (1928), "Über die Todesstrafe" (1928), "Das echte Gespräch und die Möglichkeiten des Friedens" (1953), "Haltet ein!" (1957), "Zur Ethik der politischen Entscheidung" (1932), "Zum Problem der 'Gesinnungsgemeinschaft' (1951), "Zur Klärung des Pazifismus" (1939), "November" (1948),

"Gruss und Willkomm" (1960), "Weltraumfahrt" (1957), "Danksagung" (1958), "Nach dem Tod" (1927). Previously published only in English: "Gemeinschaft und Umwelt" ("Foreword" to Eric Gutkind, *Community and Environment*, 1953), "Uber den 'bürgerlichen Ungehorsam' " (in *The Massachusetts Review. A Centenary Gathering for Henry David Thoreau*, 1962), "Nochmals über den 'bügerlichen Ungehorsam' " (in *A Matter of Life*, edited by Clara Urquhart. London: Jonathan Cape, 1963.).

Not previously published: "In Heidelberg" (1964), "weisst du es noch . . . ?" (1949), "Erinnerung an Hammarskjöld" (1962), "Über Leo Schestow" (1964), "Chassidut" (1927), "Von der Veredelung der Welt" (1923), "Das Unbewusste" (a translation by Grete Schaeder of the notes, recorded and edited by Maurice Friedman, of the three seminars on the unconscious that Martin Buber gave for the Washington School of Psychiatry in the spring of 1957. These notes, as yet unpublished in English, form the basis for Maurice Friedman's summary of Buber's teaching on the unconscious in the eighth section of his "Introductory Essay" [Chapter I] to Buber's *The Knowledge of Man* [1965], pp. 33-39), " 'In zwanzig Jahren' " (1961), "Die Drei" (1960), "Rachman, ein ferner Geist, spricht" (1942), "Danksagung" (1963), "Zuseiten mir" (1964), "Der Fiedler" (1964), "Nachwort" (1965).

1966

Addresses on Judaism. Translated by Eva Jospe. New York: Schocken Books. Includes translation of *Reden uber Judentum* (1923) and *At the Turning* (1952).

Hasidism and Modern Man. Edited and translated with an Editor's Introduction by Maurice Friedman. New York: Harper Torchbooks (paperback).

The Kingship of God. Translated by Richard Scheimann. New York: Harper & Row (*Konigtum Gottes*).

The Knowledge of Man. Edited with an Introductory Essay (Chap. I) by Maurice Friedman. Translated by Maurice Friedman and Ronald Gregor Smith. New York: Harper & Row (hardback) and Harper Torchbooks (paperback). (For contents see under 1965.)

The Origin and Meaning of Hasidism. Edited and translated with an Editor's Introduction by Maurice Friedman. New York: Harper Torchbooks (paperback).